What they're say

Very rarely does a person come along whose past life was filled with every kind of self-destructive behavior that can be imagined, yet somehow turns their life around from a place of hopelessness and prison to a place of peace and freedom.

Doug Pollock is one such person. In *Why Not Me!*, Doug begins by giving us one defining moment after another that led him to addictions, convictions, and a future destined to be spent imprisoned spiritually, mentally, and physically.

He then goes on to tell the most inspiring part of his life and journey. For the past 11 years, I have been privileged to be a part of that, counseling and mentoring Doug along the way. I can attest that when you read the second half of his book, though it may seem hard to believe, it's all true! I was there and have seen, with my own eyes, God's favor and abundant blessings that have completely changed the course of Doug's life.

No matter where you have been or what you have done, no matter where you are right now, you will be truly inspired to take a look at your own life and like Doug, say "Why Not Me!"

DR. KEVIN J. FINLEY
DDS, West Monroe, LA

Reading about a man who was sentenced to hard labor, forgotten and misplaced by society, and branded a criminal and dealer—only to become a leader and healer is a story we do not often hear. We are taught that these men who involve themselves with "those people" are not fit for polite society, and they do not deserve our time, effort, or energy.

Yet despite stumbling time and again, and despite a life often characterized by missing the mark, Doug Pollock sought forgiveness, compassion, and a new beginning. Ultimately, he transformed himself into the man of character and compassion he was always meant to be.

The life story of Doug Pollock is one of true redemption.

MICHAEL B. WRIGHT, M.D.
Psychiatrist and medical director,
Archer Institute Behavioral Health Unit,
Lake Charles, LA

This book is an exciting pathway of how God's power and grace can take a broken and hopeless case by the world's standards and turn him into a successful, humble leader—one that not only gets his own life on track but devotes his whole career to robbing back from the enemy of addiction.

I've watched Doug from the day he got out of prison and walked into a halfway house, and then rose from manager at McDonalds to starting a rehab from nothing. I was there when he met his wife and had his kids. He has held true to his recovery and beliefs and is an inspiration to all who are hopeless as well as to businessmen who feel stalled. Doug has stayed "clean shaven," positive, energetic, and always has a smile on his face, even in the tough times of life.

I endorse *Why Not Me!* because I see a person sitting in jail having *no* hope reading this book and sparking a belief in a God who has NO limits. I believe it can be a tool to bring new drive to a businessman or a father ready to give up and walk away from it all. This book is entertaining, practical, and divinely inspired.

P.S. I don't quite understand how he got it into a PG version. I can't wait to see the R-rated sequel.

DONNIE WILLIAMS
President, DRP Masonry, LLC, Monroe, LA

In his book *Why Not Me!* my dear friend Doug Pollock delivers a true testament of God's heart. He invites you into a world of destruction, lies, and chaos, one where lives and destinies are on the brink of despair and disaster . . . BUT GOD! He makes a way!

A godly man with passions like yours, Doug lives daily by the creed, "Why Not Me!" His desire is to see people transformed by God's great redeeming love, and this book was birthed out of that desire. Doug has an unshakeable and undeniable trust in God's plan for his life—and yours.

You will be left saying, "I have to have more" when you finish this poignant and exceptional book. Journey with Doug and his lovely wife, Kristin, as they walk through tremendous, heart-wrenching situations, and see how their God answers. You, too, can say, "Why Not Me!"

TERESA GROCE
Former host of the television program
"Designed For Destiny," West Monroe, LA

When I first started reading *Why Not Me!*, I had initially thought that I would just skim through it for a few minutes and then come back to it later. After nearly two hours, I realized that I had been completely immersed in the story. In short, Doug Pollock's book is compelling, interesting, and quite insightful. The clarity of expression, coupled with the depth of thought, make for an easy read that, paradoxically, leads to very deep contemplation.

Going further, Doug shows how the work of God can open our hearts to achieve a sense of purpose, peace, and serenity. He provides a story that shows how even the most difficult of life's circumstances can, oddly enough, be our most rewarding experiences; in adversity we can find ourselves, and we can find purpose.

Doug shares how his marital journey with his wife, Kristin, has provided a multidimensional view of life that goes well beyond that of an individual perspective. Together, they demonstrate how a Scripture-based walk through life can provide an enormous sense of realization and belonging. Their story provides enrichment toward a life of quality, happiness, and hope that is inspiring to anyone who considers their message.

ROBERT D. HANSER, PH.D.
Professor and Clinician, West Monroe, LA

WHY *Not* ME!

Find the courage to change the definition of your life

Doug Pollock with Kristin Pollock

Monroe, LA

Why Not Me!
by Doug Pollock
© 2021 by Doug Pollock. All rights reserved.

Editing by Adam Colwell's WriteWorks, LLC,
    Adam Colwell and Ginger Colwell
Cover and book design by Clarity Designworks
Published by Adam Colwell's WriteWorks, LLC
Printed in the United States of America
ISBN (Paperback): 978-1-7371711-1-9
ISBN (eBook): 978-1-7371711-2-6

CONTENTS

Acknowledgements xi

Foreword: John Skipworth xiii

Note from the Author xv

Prologue: Where Success Begins xvii

CHAPTER ONE:
Doug Pollock's Long Day Off 1

CHAPTER TWO:
Set Up and Sent Down 19

CHAPTER THREE:
Stuck on Stupid 39

CHAPTER FOUR:
Bottoming Out 59

CHAPTER FIVE:
Nowhere to Go but Up 81

Photo Gallery 105

CHAPTER SIX:
Free at Last—or Was I? 129

CHAPTER SEVEN:
I Finally Found It 145

CHAPTER EIGHT:
Love, Marriage—and Secrets Exposed 167

CHAPTER NINE:
Finding Your New Day 187

CHAPTER TEN:
Defining Moments and a "New" New Day 209

To my late friend, Dennis Washington, who I met while I was in prison. I believe that the man you were when you came to prison was nothing like the man you were when you left prison. I will honor your memory and good name all the days of my life.

To every one of you hanging on to THE HOPE that sets you free. Don't let go!

ACKNOWLEDGEMENTS

It is my belief that our lives are comprised from our defining moments. Some are obvious, others maybe not so much. As I have had the privilege of going back and reviewing many of those defining moments, I realized that I was living with the wrong definition of me because I did not know who I was created to be.

The good news is that there were many people who chose to see me, through the eyes of faith, as the person I would become if I could change my self-belief. These people chose to believe in me when I couldn't believe in myself, which is a beautiful illustration of God's goodness and mercy.

To Ms. Waters, my tenth-grade English teacher; Mr. Carl Morrow, my adult Sunday School teacher in Baton Rouge, Louisiana; and Michael Robison and Darla O'Connor, who stood by me through my incarceration—you are all examples of people who may never know the outcome of my life this side of eternity but were instrumental in my life.

Then there are other people who kept believing in me, and even poured of themselves into my life to squeeze out more of what they knew was in me. Kathy Biedenharn and Ricky Banks of City of Faith are two of these people. Kathy personally took me to job interviews, and after I'd get a job and realize it wasn't for me, she say, "Well, where should we try next?"

To Corodney Specks, Angela Matthews, Dr. Susan Tucker, and Warden Batson—while I was in prison, you treated me with kindness and respect in an environment where it's about breaking you down in order to teach you a lesson. Even though the back of every shirt I wore was labeled DOC# 319754, I had chosen to carry myself like I was not a prisoner, and I truly believe each of you secretly hoped, and maybe even knew, that my prisoner number did not have the power to define who I was.

To Tony Gilley, an owner and operator of multiple McDonalds, and my supervisors, Jennifer and Darren— I have realized you had a plan to train and promote me, and the time that I worked for you was so monumental in my transition from prison to the free world.

To my mentor and friend, Dr. Kevin Finley—you opened a door and gave me an invitation to join you on a journey of transformation to become a man who would lead a family, guide multiple businesses, and have a heart and mind that would become more and more in sync with God's opinion of me.

Let me not forget Mr. Danny Prince and the great trust he extended to me from the very beginning. I will ever be grateful for the love of a Christian businessman who changed the course of my life forever.

Last, but most important, are my wife and my kids. You allow me to be the most important person in this world to you. I daily walk out what I believe is the greatest blessing ever in being husband, daddy, best friend, coach, teacher, and any other hat I get to wear for you. Together, we are building one defining moment after another that will carry a legacy to last many lifetimes.

FOREWORD

Why Not Me! is not only a great title, but it is also a revelation most of us never recognize during the course of our
lives. This is often because so many of us tend to think too
little of ourselves, our lives, and our purpose. As a pastor and
teacher of the Bible for over two decades, I would strongly
say that this lack of purpose in our lives flows out of a pre-
dominately incorrect viewpoint of God's love and desires for
His creation.

In this captivating, life-changing, tell-all book, my dear
friend, Doug Pollock, shares his story. It's a tale of brokenness,
pain, tragedy, bankruptcy, prison, conversion, restoration,
purpose, and so much more.

This is a story I personally know because I was there
through much of his journey. Doug and I have been through
the valleys and mountaintops of life. I have watched as a
friend, a supporter, and a confidant as Doug's life transformed. This story is book-worthy, movie-worthy, and
your-lifeworthy. You need to hear it, digest it, believe it, and
receive it for yourself.

Regardless of your view, this book is going to force you
to ask yourself, "Why not me?" regarding God's purposes,
will, and destiny for you, and exclaim, like Doug so often

did, "Why not me!" You will be encouraged, inspired, and astonished by all God can and will do in your life.

Doug's story is sincere, compelling, raw, and riveting. Even more, this book will challenge you and prayerfully transform you. I encourage you to read it and then proclaim, "Why not me!"

What do you have to lose? Better yet, what do you have to gain?

JOHN SKIPWORTH,
Lead Pastor of Oaks Church,
Monroe, Louisiana

Note from the Author

The events and accounts depicted in this book are related as best as I remember them. In some cases, I chose not to use an individual's actual name to protect their identity. I also did my best to not misrepresent any person or incident in any way.

———

WHERE SUCCESS BEGINS

THE DAY I WENT TO COURT for my final hearing, I had a pretty good idea what was about to take place.

That's probably why what happened next was such a surprise.

The lights in the courtroom were dim, casting a soft, dreary glow over the dark woodgrains of the desks, rails, and the bench behind which sat the older, salt and pepper-haired judge who was about to hand down my sentence. Others were there: the attorneys, the bailiff, and those waiting to be sentenced after me. But it was as if the black-robed judge and I were the only people there. I had tunnel vision, and everyone else on the periphery was blurry and, therefore, rendered unimportant.

I shuffled, causing the shackles around my feet to jangle. I must've surely cast a striking picture, standing there handcuffed and wearing the familiar orange jumpsuit of the incarcerated.

I knew it had already been determined that if I waived my rights to a trial and pled guilty, all but one of the charges against me were going to be dropped. That would reduce my 30-year sentence to 20, with the first 10 years spent in prison before, should all go well, the rest of the term was served out on parole.

Never in my life did I think I would be so willing to accept a fate of spending the next decade behind bars. Several months earlier, I'd told my attorney I wasn't taking a two-year sentence, much less a 20-year term. That obviously didn't happen.

I guess that was understandable considering why I was arrested: possession of cocaine, possession of benzodiazepines (a depressant like Xanax or Valium), possession of gamma hydroxybutyrate (better known as GHB, another depressant), and possession of marijuana, all with the intent to distribute. It wasn't the first time I'd been busted, but the fact that I was done in by a reverse sting operation, one where the people I bought drugs from ratted on me, especially sucked. When they insisted we meet at my business, I agreed to do it. Normally, to protect myself, I met with someone at their house.

But I didn't do it that way, it was stupid, and now I was getting ready to pay for it.

Dearly.

Yet when the judge declared my sentence, the very one I knew was coming, I suddenly felt as though I was having an out-of-body experience. I was locked in to what the judge was saying, but I was also swept away as some sort of strange, new courage penetrated my being. Entered my heart.

I realized this wasn't the end. It was something else entirely. A new beginning.

"Okay," I said quietly to myself. "This is gonna be okay."

I didn't know at all what "okay" actually meant. I just knew the dude had given me a 20-year sentence and I was *good*. I wasn't sad or depressed or tearful. I had a peace that something was going to come out of it all.

By then, I had been reading the Bible for a while, and I was definitely familiar with that passage in Philippians about the peace of God that surpasses all understanding. But at that moment, I think it was also a relief that the sentencing was over. I knew my fate, and I had accepted it.

A huge weight had been removed from my shoulders and my mind. It was totally unexpected.

The judge read his final statement confirming that I hadn't been coerced or promised anything in return for the plea bargain, then asked me if I had anything to say.

Who in the world would have anything to say out loud after that besides "ouch?" I thought.

But I did have something to say. Actually, I told him I had two things to say.

"You just gave me a 20-year sentence. I'm going to be sent to the Louisiana Department of Corrections to serve my time doing hard labor," I began respectfully. "I am going to prison, but I'm not going to be serving time. That time is going to serve me. I'm not going to waste one single day while I'm there, and I will make the most of every opportunity. I am going to learn all that I can and be a success story for you."

The judge looked at me, chuckled, and said, "Thanks, Mr. Pollock," as he waved for me to be escorted out of the court.

"I still have one more thing I wanted to say," I politely reminded him, then continued. "Not only am I going to prison to not serve time but for time to serve me, but I'm going to spend every day I'm there trying to figure out how to get out of this 20-year sentence."

He did a lot more than chuckle at that. It was a full-on belly laugh. "Good luck!" he declared.

At that moment, I believed I could have a 20-year prison sentence and still be *successful*. It was there that I began a journey of challenging the normal thought processes that saw problems and difficulties as obstacles, and I shifted my thinking to see them as opportunities and blessings.

It wasn't cockiness. It wasn't arrogance. It wasn't even being naïve. It was the start of a mindset change—one that would end up carrying me for years to come and ultimately change my life.

Most people would readily agree that 20 years of hard labor is anything but an opportunity, let alone a blessing. But people living at varying levels of success know that they had to say "yes" to things that are hard to do. "Yes" to things that would stretch them and their minds to find solutions buried deep within them.

I have come to understand that real success is not measured by a big office or a hefty salary (the result or the outcome), but in the decisions and the actions that follow as you face situations that are difficult and out of the norm.

Success starts when you see the obstacle as an opportunity, and it develops as you move toward the destiny before you.

CHAPTER ONE

DOUG POLLOCK'S
LONG DAY OFF

I WISH I COULD TELL YOU that the next 10 years of my life were easy. I certainly can't say that. But I can say that those 10 years were not only some of the best of my life up to that point, they were also the years that began to shape me into a person I never knew existed.

Up until then, the person I'd always known was pretty much a mess.

Oh, I was smart. I was in all the advanced or gifted classes in school. But my high school principal nailed it when he said, "You know who you remind me of? Ferris Bueller. You're smart enough to excel academically, but cunning enough to get around the fringes of what you're supposed to do, for the most part, without getting caught."

He was right about that—but unlike Ferris and his fictional day off, I rarely stopped. By then, I'd been using and dealing for a long time. In junior high, I was kicked out of the Dallas, Texas Independent School District and had to go to neighboring Louisiana to attend school because I was super rebellious, skipping school, smoking pot, and hanging out with all the wrong kids.

It got out of control from there.

Some of that was probably me being a seventh-grade, 13-year-old punk wanting to get high and do his own thing. But my mom and dad were divorced by then, too, so that was a factor. Not an excuse, mind you, but a factor.

From the time I can first remember, my parents were going at each other, especially if they'd been drinking. We lived in Mesquite, a suburb of Dallas, Texas. Dad, Barry, was a psychologist; mom, Diane, stayed home to raise me and my two siblings, older sister, Penny, and younger brother, Mark. Oddly enough, mom and dad also worked for a while at a children's home, and it was nothing for them to take in stray kids, teens all the way up to young adults, even after my parent's marital problems caused them to separate.

On one such occasion, my mom had agreed to watch a baby belonging to the friends of one of those strays. She had already kept the child for a while when the baby fell ill. Mom contacted a pediatrician and was recommended a medication. However, the supplier of the medication had kept it too long and much of it had evaporated, leaving it with a dosage that was too concentrated. My mom gave it to the baby and went away for a while, leaving the infant in the care of my 13-year-old sister.

When she returned, she found that the baby had died. Penny had no clue anything was wrong until mom came home and discovered the child unconscious, right there in the crib.

Mom called dad, then contacted the police. She was arrested that night, right in front of my eyes. She was deemed as being at fault and went to jail.

The next day, our entire family got together: Mark, Penny, my dad, and both of my grandparents. Everyone was trying to figure out how to raise the money needed to get her out on bail.

I reached into my pocket and pulled out two quarters. Fifty cents. It was all I had.

When I handed it to my dad, everyone fell apart. They were so sad and desperate to get her out of jail as soon as they could.

She didn't get out for over two months, not until Christmas Eve. It took that long to prove what had really happened with the medication.

In the interim, my brother and sister and I stayed with my grandmother. I think that was because we had to sell our house in order to get her out. I don't really remember what I got that Christmas under the tree, but it was a happy time. I know everyone tried to shield us kids from what was going on. They tried to make it as normal a Christmas as they possibly could.

Normal wasn't really a part of my childhood from then on.

~~~~

Even though mom was eventually cleared of any wrongdoing with the baby's death, the incident didn't help my parent's already tattered relationship. Their marriage went from bad to worse. They drank more and began using speed. Mom was more or less a closet alcoholic. She often enjoyed a glass of orange juice with vodka in it. Dad just drank beer, but there were definitely times he'd have so much that he spent the entire day buzzed. I didn't see anything wrong with it and sometimes tried to nab a sip of beer myself.

I saw my mom shooting up, and there were times they made drug deal runs to get their stuff. My parents tried to be discreet, but as kids, we always knew. We were more intuitive than we were given credit for. Most children are. Mark was two years younger than me, and we were typical bratty brothers. Best buddies, we got along with Penny but didn't at the same time. There was just too much of an age difference between us and her. I was like a parent to my brother. I always looked out for Mark and was very protective of him.

When they were together, mom and dad argued most of the time. There was a lot of verbal abuse and even a little pushing and shoving. The fact that we were faithful Sunday morning attendees of First Baptist Church in downtown Dallas didn't seem to make much difference. I did enjoy going to church. It was a positive place, even the day I was scolded by my dad for yelling, "Stop, doo-doo head!" to the driver of a car coming at us as we walked across the street after service. I got my butt tore up for that; ironic, considering the way he was behaving the rest of the week.

Part of that behavior included adultery. In fact, both of my parents were cheating on each other before and after their separation. It wasn't a secret. In fact, it was the main thing they argued about. Again, all of us kids knew it was happening. Since we were with mom most of the time, we couldn't help but notice. We'd go places with her and sometimes end up somewhere we probably weren't supposed to be because she was meeting up with the person she was seeing, Apparently, she had a specific boyfriend. Dad didn't so much have a girlfriend. He saw different women.

This continued as we moved to Wichita Falls, Texas, where we rented a home. That was the last place our family was together before the drugs, drinking, and infidelity took their toll and mom and dad split up. I had my seventh birthday there, and we lived in that home for about nine months before returning to Dallas with mom so that we could live with our Aunt Debbie.

A thin, petite, pretty blonde, Aunt Debbie was my mother's sister. She lived near our grandparents and brought a sense of stability to our tumultuous lives. It was just the basics: going to school when we were supposed to, regular mealtimes, that sort of thing. But it helped.

A public-school teacher with no children of her own at the time, Aunt Debbie had a positive influence on us. It wasn't easy for her. Her husband was a pilot and lived far away in San Antonio, Texas, so he came back and forth when he could. But Aunt Debbie still took care of us as if we were her own. She'd always have cut up celery sticks and carrots in a bowl of water in the icebox for us to have as snacks. She was diabetic, so she tried to help us eat healthy things. Any time I think of my aunt I recall those snacks, and I still love celery and carrots to this day.

Aunt Debbie was amazing and a good, Christian woman. We always tagged along when she taught Vacation Bible School during the summers. In fact, the very first trophy I ever won was for memorizing Bible verses at one of her classes when I was nine. Our time living with Aunt Debbie was a precious pocket of time, a bit of normalcy in the midst of the chaos. She exposed us to a way of life that I'd later come to admire and want to emulate. She provided routine and structure along with a sense of family that I would draw from years later as I started my own family.

My parents, meanwhile, went their separate ways. Dad went far away to Orange, Texas, east of Houston near the Louisiana border, to live with his parents for a year-and-a-half to try to get his life on track. We saw dad around the holidays, Christmas, or during the summer, and we talked to him every now and then on the phone. Mom was with us and helped take care of us when she wasn't at work. I don't remember her ever having a full-time job, but she was extremely artistic and talented. She could paint and draw, and there were numerous times she'd hustle up small jobs at local businesses painting a sign or decorating the window so she could get school shoe money for us.

With my parents apart, there wasn't any chaos going on. Life was okay, and for the next 18 months living with my aunt, we settled into a new normal. I got by as good as could be expected—not knowing things were about to get a lot harder.

~~~~~

When Aunt Debbie decided it would be best for her marriage if she moved to San Antonio to be with her husband, we were on the move again, this time just a couple of blocks away to our grandparent's house. By then I was nine, and my Grandma Allyne (she was my mom's mother, and we called her My Ma) maintained the stability Aunt Debbie had provided with regular meals, school attendance, and church, where we learned all the stories from the Old Testament. Grandma sold real estate, and we'd have fun going out with her to the houses.

My Ma was also a good, Christian lady who expected us to behave accordingly, and I did my best. I went to the summer church camps, was an honor student in school, and generally kept myself out of trouble.

As far as mom and dad were concerned, they finally got a divorce when I was ten. It was finalized on my Uncle Carlton's birthday, and I happened to be at his house. That was the first day I ever got drunk. He had Bartles & Jaymes wine coolers, and I downed four of them. It was his weird way of celebrating his birthday while also drowning out the divorce. That was also the first time I learned what "hugging the toilet" meant.

By then, dad had found a job in Louisiana and moved to New Orleans close to the French Quarter. I was such a daddy's boy. From the time I was little I remember hiding in the back of a motor home that belonged to my grandparents that dad stayed in whenever my mom and dad weren't getting along. One morning he was getting ready to drive to work in the motor home, and I hid in the tiny bathroom in the cabin. Just after he pulled out to leave, I crept out and plopped down right next to him. It practically scared him out of the driver's seat, and he had to turn around and take me back home. I did stuff like that just so I could be near him.

I always wanted to stay with my dad, visit my dad, or move in with my dad. I missed him tremendously. But mom protected me from my father, not because she was intentionally trying to keep me away from him, but because she didn't want my feelings to get hurt. Fact was, she knew my dad was not able to take care of me or raise me living as a single man in New Orleans.

Then, right around the end of fifth grade, My Ma had a falling out with mom. I don't recall what it was about, but it probably had to do with mom's drinking. It had escalated since the divorce, and she was starting to show the early signs of the liver disease that would take her life years later. My Ma was also not happy that mom was still seeing her boyfriend who managed the liquor store where my mother bought her alcohol. There was one time my brother and I were with her at his apartment. We went away to the video arcade, but when we returned and knocked on the door, he opened it and let us in—just to kick my brother in the back of the head before grabbing me by the hair and flinging me across the room. I think he was drunk and probably angry because we were banging on the door. There was no telling what we may have interrupted. Mom was pissed, grabbed us up, and got us out of there, and Mark and I only saw him a couple of times after that. That was the only time he put his hands on us like that, but it was enough. He was definitely an asshole. We didn't care for him.

So, to not have to hear My Ma tell her what to do anymore, and probably just to prove a point, my stubborn mom packed us up and moved us out. We settled in an apartment complex a couple of miles away from grandma's house in a not-so-good, lower income, racially mixed part of Dallas. It was near a major intersection and had 150-200 units with doors and stoops all in big rows next to one another. It wasn't a crap hole, but it wasn't first-class living, either. We weren't there long before mom was diagnosed with cirrhosis of the liver. As mom's legs and belly started to swell from the disease, we had to start helping her go to the bathroom and stay hydrated. Normal went quickly out the window.

It was also there where I first started hanging out in the woods behind the complex with some kids that I had no business being with. We'd sneak off to smoke cigarettes or joints, and we'd grab some alcohol if we could. One of those kids was Todd. A year older than me and with a brother several years older than him, Todd and I hit it off. Skinny, he had a few freckles on his nose and brownish hair with a little red in it. He tried to be cool with his Cavaricci parachute pants and Members Only zip up black jacket. We walked to and from school together most of the time.

By the time sixth grade ended, we were back with our grandmother, likely because of mom's fading health and My Ma wanting to get us back into a better environment. But the negative influence of my new friends followed me there. One day, when Todd stole pot from his older brother, I took money from My Ma and gave it to him so I could have a bit of the stash. I was scared and nervous, and I hoped I wouldn't get caught because I knew it would hurt her feelings and that I'd get into big trouble. But none of that stopped me.

It was my very first drug transaction.

I was 12.

I can't say there was a specific motivation to my choices. I don't think my self-esteem was high, but no one was telling me I had to do it, and I wasn't acting out because my mother was ill. It was as simple as everybody else did it, I tried it, and I liked it.

That's all it took.

I went to Louisiana for about eight weeks that summer to visit my father, and I made some friends while I was there who smoked pot with me. After my return to Dallas to begin seventh grade, I started hanging around with other older kids from junior high whose parents drank, smoked dope, and sold it, too. I drank on Fridays and Saturdays—no hard stuff, just Budweiser Long Necks, even if I hated how they tasted— but my main thing was marijuana. I smoked weed every day in the alleys before and after school, and I sold joints during school. Back then, students were labeled as a prep, a head, or a jock. I was definitely a head, meaning a pot head.

I began missing classes, so much so that I got an NG ("no grade") on my report card. Whenever we skipped school for the day, usually right after first period, we went to a place called "The Swing." It was a big bowl-like area in the woods carved out of a grove of trees that surrounded it and a white rock creek bed that meandered through it with just enough water to get our shoes wet. Several of the trees had ropes hanging down from the branches, and we'd go out there, high as a kite, and swing, do crazy tricks, and try to outperform one another with our antics.

It was at age 13 when I also began using cocaine. I didn't do it often, usually on a Friday or Saturday at the house of a friend whose parents sold it. Just like you see in the movies, we'd lay out the powder on the table in thin, straight lines and snort it up through a straw. Even then, I knew cocaine was very addictive. It didn't take much to teach me that, and the highs never lasted long enough. They always faded away, leaving me trying to figure out how to get back to where I had been. It was far different from the low, mellow buzz I got from marijuana. Pot didn't amp me up. It was a depressant, so it made me a little sillier. More stupid.

I thought that my experiences with alcohol and drugs were good, but in reality, they weren't. I remember missing lunch at home after walking miles to a friend's house on a clear but bitterly cold Christmas Day to go buy some cocaine. I ended up getting there, staying too long, and missing the meal. Who wouldn't feel guilty for missing Christmas lunch because they were snorting coke? I guarantee my family suspected and probably knew that I was smoking pot on a regular basis. I'm sure they suspected the drinking, too, but not the cocaine use. I didn't do that all the time. Normally, that was easier to hide since I'd be at a friend's house, and I made sure I came home after everyone was asleep.

I hustled jobs like crazy during junior high. I had my first formal job working at a plastic factory for $3.00 an hour after school making trifold plastic picture frames. I was always trying to sneak away with the lawn mower and hedger to go mow somebody's yard. I worked in restaurants bussing tables or washing dishes. I worked in fast food. I did anything and everything as often as I could to get money to buy drugs.

It finally caught up to me at school midway through seventh grade. I was in the hallway trying to sell some pot to a classmate, and he and I got into an altercation. A teacher tried to intervene and almost got hit in the fight. I was blamed and promptly sent to the principal's office. With all my skipping of classes, they had already told me that if I got one more bang against me, my school career was over for the year. I was given two choices. One was to get five licks with the paddle; the other was to be kicked out of school. I chose expulsion.

It was self-sabotage to some degree because I knew I could now likely get permission to go live with my dad in Louisiana. Mom couldn't handle me anymore, and her health was only getting worse. On the other hand, by that time dad was remarried, stable, and had a support system. He had also gone to work as a licensed professional counselor with the State of Louisiana. I arrived at his house at the end of January, right before Mardi Gras. My father literally had to go to the principal in St. Tammany Parish to petition to get me back in school. He proposed that they let me go to school there on the condition I made straight A's the rest of the year, and they said yes.

My father, with my stepmom's help, laid down the law. I didn't put up too much of a fuss. I attended school every day, didn't ditch, and every night I had to go in my room for two hours without getting on the phone or watching TV. They couldn't make me study, but since I *had* to be in there, I did—and I was able to complete seventh grade on time.

My stepmom was Christine, and I quickly grew to like her. A nurse, she was pretty much black and white. She wasn't going to settle for any type of foolishness from my dad, probably because her first marriage wasn't the best. Early on in their relationship, my dad made a comment about taking her out to a local place where they played music. In south Louisiana, everything is a bar. Christine told him, "I don't want to go to places like that. If you want to go to places like that, you won't be going with me." My dad responded, "No, I guess I really don't like those places so much." He should've known. After all, he'd met her in an adult singles Sunday school class at church where she served on the committee that greeted all the new folks.

When I first met Christine, I thought, "Who's this lady trying to take my mom's spot? She even has a daughter." But she didn't try to be my mom at all. She was just there for me. She was a really good woman. When I moved to Louisiana, I had long hair and dressed like a dopehead. Christine and my father didn't make me get a haircut, but she did take me out to get some new clothes. I went from raggedy t-shirts and tank tops to pullovers and polos. We realized we liked to go shopping together, and Christine somehow connected with me in ways my dad didn't and that my mother never had.

The makeover eventually led me to get my hair cut. It was around that time when puberty was really kicking in, and I wanted to do something to change mentally and emotionally. I cut back on the alcohol and drugs, at least at first. I was working at my friend's dad's restaurant in Slidell, and I'd sneak a beer every now and then. I didn't smoke any dope right off the bat, although I ultimately went on the hunt to discover who did what around there. When I went to Dallas for the summer and hung out with my old friends, I began drinking and using once more, so by the time I returned to Louisiana, my brief season of change was over.

I'd been given a fresh start, but I was beginning to mess it up.

~~~~

There was an undeveloped neighborhood behind the subdivision where we lived. It was there I met Belinda, a girl I went to school with whose dad had some of the best pot in the parish. She wasn't a girlfriend, just a fellow dopehead, but we hooked up, and I started buying, using, and eventually selling some of the prize weed to eleventh graders who knew they couldn't get it anywhere else but through me. Somehow, I always sniffed out the best connections. Dad always said I could come in one side of town and would have met every wrong person I could before I came out the other side. In the meantime, I kept the same routine at home, sequestered in my room each school night, and I managed to keep my grades up, though I wasn't doing as much homework as I had before. I didn't skip school as much either because I knew I'd get kicked out.

It was strange at first learning to live with my stepsister, Aimee. At first, I had an underlying twinge of territorial jealousy toward her, mostly a, "That is not your dad. That is my dad" sort of thing. But she was younger, and we were closer in age. We were only four years apart, far different than my real sister, Penny, who was almost seven years older than me. Therefore, Aimee and I soon started getting along much like a typical brother and sister. I irritated her, she irritated me, but no one was allowed to irritate her but me. One time, some neighborhood kid was picking on her, and I ended up punching him smack in the mouth. He lost some teeth, and I got in trouble, but no one was going to bother Aimee if I was around.

During the summer I went to Dallas again for a while and then returned to Louisiana with my brother, Mark, for a few more weeks before he returned to Texas for school. Mark and I were close, my wrestling and football buddy. I took him everywhere with me. We were real mischievous, too, just like Frick and Frack. It was like we had never been apart when he was in Louisiana with me. We'd sneak away in dad's car during the day and go out onto the back, gravel roads to drink a little and smoke some pot. Because of mom's drinking problem, the only time Mark actually had alcohol was with me. I was a bad influence on him that was only going to get worse.

Mark didn't have much of a problem with Aimee, or her with him. That was okay. Mark and I didn't have a lot to do with Penny at that point. She had been gone from mom's house for a while by then, out on her own, doing speed, and dancing at topless clubs. Her and I talked on the phone sometimes, and when I went to Dallas, I took time to hang out with her. But that was about it.

I managed to keep up my good boy act at home while drinking, and using and selling drugs, on the side. I stayed nicely under the radar until the inevitable happened. It was in ninth grade, my first year in high school. I was in wood-shop, and I told the teacher that I needed to run out to my car to get an excuse note to turn in to the principal for being absent the day before. The excuse, of course, was a lie; I had ditched the previous day. While I was at the car, a little AMC Spirit hatchback, I got in and smoked a joint with the windows cracked. I thought I'd be letting out just enough of the odoriferous smoke to not be noticed while making sure there wasn't enough of the reek on my clothes to give me away.

When I arrived at the principal's office (the same principal who'd previously declared that I was like Ferris Bueller in how I could get around the fringes of what I was supposed to do), he took a good whiff.

"You smell like marijuana," he stated.

"Marijuana?" I feigned my shock at the audacity of the accusation. "Marijuana? I don't smoke marijuana?"

He smirked and began patting me down, starting on my left side under my arms. Swiftly, I grabbed a handful of joints I had stuffed into my right jacket pocket and deftly shoved them into my pants pocket. When he patted down the right side, he could smell their residue on my coat but missed finding the hidden evidence.

He then took me into his office, and I was thinking, *Should I jump out the window? Run?*

That was when I realized I was sitting in a box spring chair. I scooted it up close to the principal's desk and placed my left arm on the desk in front of me while I slid my other arm down the side and began urgently ripping a hole in the upholstery. I tried to cover up the noise and distract him with my best "woe is me" pitch, and as quickly as I could, I snagged the joints out of my pants and stuffed them into the hole I'd just made in the chair.

Deed done, I leaned back, and the principal didn't seem to have noticed anything. I couldn't believe it. *I think I got away with this.*

I thought I was so clever, and I must've told a few folks about it, because right after last period was over, the principal called me back to his office.

"I've had more people in here today getting in trouble, and then I heard from someone that you had put some joints in my chair." He gestured toward it, the stepped over and flipped it upside down. Sure enough, there was the hole I'd made, but nothing was in it. The joints were gone.

I never found out what happened to them, and I denied everything, of course, but it didn't work.

I got suspended for ten days.

As punishment, and in an attempt to keep an eye on me, my dad made me go with him to the Desire Projects, a notorious public housing development in the Ninth Ward of New Orleans, where he was offering counseling services to the residents on behalf of the state. I accompanied him for a week, and my behavior was so bad he couldn't stand it. I tried to sneak off to smoke pot whenever I could. That's how stupid I was. My father was so frustrated he made me stay home the next week.

I didn't look at what I was doing as disobeying him. I was just going to do what I wanted.

That was in January. Later in the semester, I was outside picking up trash in the courtyard at school between the two wings right outside the principal's office. One of the screens was off one of the windows, and I put one foot on one end, lifted it up, and bent it. I was thinking, *I'll teach them to make me do this,* but I was really just being destructive for the sake of being destructive.

It just so happened the principal was looking right at me through his office window. I got suspended five days for that.

I first tried Ecstasy during the ninth grade when I stayed at a friend's house over the weekend. We'd usually head over to a club in New Orleans and stay up all night. During the summer between ninth and tenth grades, all I did was smoke pot and eat Ecstasy like it was candy. It was also during this time that I began using LSD, but I preferred Ecstasy. When you take Ecstasy, it's called "rolling." It makes you feel real good, like you love everyone. When I went to Dallas, I even gave some to Mark for the first time.

Back in school for tenth grade, I got busted for having pot at school, just like I had the year before. I had also started hanging out during afternoons and on weekends with kids from Southeastern Louisiana University. At home, I routinely disregarded the rules. I kept drinking, kept doping, and kept doing whatever I pleased.

I was beginning to spiral.

By the time the school year ended, I had missed just enough school to be one credit short of being able to advance.

But that wasn't the worst thing that happened as May rolled around.

I was working at a fast food restaurant, and I had come home one Friday afternoon to do my laundry. For whatever reason, I always wanted my clothes to be clean. My stepmom was elsewhere in the house when my dad came up to me after he got home from work.

"I'll bet you've already spent your whole paycheck from work," he said.

He knew it was payday, and he was checking up on me. But his snide remark made it sound like I was being irresponsible with my money—or, at least, that's the way I heard it.

"No," I shot back. "I've got my paycheck right here!"

I grabbed for my front jeans pocket where my check was located, but he must've thought I was grabbing for my crotch and making an obscene gesture of disrespect toward him.

Out of nowhere, my father jumped me, putting his hands around my neck. I got away from the hold and pushed him away, but we both automatically made our way outside to the front yard.

"You want to fight?" he asked in a tone that certainly suggested that he was more than ready for a brawl. We had spent the past three-and-a-half years taking taekwondo together, practicing everything a fighter used in competitions. We were both black belts, so we knew how to handle ourselves.

"Yeah! Let me take my necklace off." It was just a little gold chain, nothing special, but I didn't want it to get broken.

As I reached my hands behind my neck, he popped me in the mouth.

My dad just punched me! I thought. I couldn't help but feel like I did when I was about to get into a fight with some kid I didn't like.

"Man, that was cold blooded!" I yelled, my response muffled by the blow.

I grabbed him and tussled him to the ground. I got him in a hold where both of our butts were in the air, but my arms were wrapped around his midsection. I was on top of him in a way that made sure he couldn't move around, hit me, or kick me. My youth and my anger got the best of my old man. But I didn't hit him or try to do anything to injure him.

"I love you," I told him, grunting. "This is crazy. We need to stop this."

Imagine me, the voice of reason at a moment like that.

I felt him become less tense in my grip. We released one another, got up, and went our separate ways. It had all happened so fast. As I went to my room to settle down, I could tell my stepmom was not at all happy with our little front yard smackdown.

Later, dad came into my room with an ultimatum. "The way I see it, you have three choices. You can stay here, live in this house, and follow the rules. We could go out in the backyard in the morning and do this again. Or you can move out."

Annoyance and pride welled within me. *You think I'm going to stay here and be a good little boy? No, that is not what I am doing. You gave me an option, and I'm going to take it.*

"I'll take number three."

It had all been building up to that. I'd been flaunting the rules all year—and I'm sure it was all building up inside of him, too.

The next day, with just my clothes in a bag, I moved in with Eric, one of my college-aged buddies. I first met Eric when I sold drugs to him. We were good friends, had held some jobs together, and I knew his family well. I spent the entire summer with him, hanging out, drinking beer, smoking pot, and doing Ecstasy.

I didn't just continue my bad behavior. I cranked it up.

I also got a job working at a boatyard building shrimp trawlers as well as fiberglass and flat-bottomed boats. I still visited my dad, stepmom, and stepsister that summer, but I didn't go to Dallas. Instead, Mark came to Louisiana. He stayed with my dad and was, therefore, sequestered to that neighborhood.

Eric and I weren't going to go along with that, though. The pair of us planned a camping trip to Mississippi and asked dad if we could take Mark with us. While he refused to let him go with us, he did give permission for Mark to camp in the nearby woods with some of the neighbors—but when Mark left our father's house, we came and took him with us to Mississippi anyway. Mark had to be back at a certain time, however, and we didn't return with him until late in the afternoon. Dad was so pissed he immediately sent Mark back home.

Then, right before school was ready to start back up in late August, dad came over to Eric's place to see me—and he delivered another ultimatum.

"It is time to come home. You've proved your point anyway. You need to come on back home."

That was it. I returned home. I ended up returning to school, too, for eleventh grade after Mrs. Waters, the English teacher whose grade was going to hold me back, decided to give me the credit I needed.

I was being given a second chance at home and at school.

Question was, what was I going to do with it?

CHAPTER TWO

———

SET UP
AND SENT DOWN

ANSWER: I WASTED IT—though it certainly didn't seem that way to me at the beginning.

I stayed at home for a month before I decided to leave home for good and move into an apartment with my girlfriend, Tammy, and another guy her and I met called "Crazy Dave." Tammy was great. She wasn't some super gorgeous, fine chick, but she was a nice girl, a pretty, skinny brunette who was about five years older than I was. I met her at one of my former employers, and she was my first love in the sense that she was my first real girlfriend. She was from Mississippi, and I wanted to be with her and have more independence. I felt I could make grown up decisions even though I was really still just a boy.

We shared a nice two-story, two-bedroom townhome-type place in a fairly good neighborhood located near a bayou that came off of Lake Pontchartrain and the U.S. 11 bridge that carried traffic from Slidell to New Orleans. I remained in school and tried to stick with it, but that was kind of hard to do when I was smoking dope and popping Ecstasy all night and then trying to get up the next morning.

My attendance dropped off, as did my studies. It wasn't long before I cleaned out my locker and dropped out. I never returned to school after that.

I continued working at the boatyard until I was fired about a month after we got the apartment. They didn't really give me a reason, but I think work was slowing down, and I was probably the least skilled person they had.

The first month my rent was due, I went to my dad's house. I told him about how my rent was $350 and I had about $250, and I asked to borrow the rest from him.

He just looked at me and said, "Welcome to the real world."

I left that day and made a promise to myself that I was never going to find myself in that situation again, and I went right to work—selling weed and Ecstasy so we could pay the rent and buy groceries.

Crazy Dave didn't help. A typical motorcycle gang-looking dude with long hair and a mustache, Dave didn't have a job, but we couldn't kick him out, either. He had just got out of prison, and he was big and buff from working out all the time. His family lived near my parents, and his sister was among my group of older friends. She had introduced me to him that previous summer. While I don't recall what he did to get behind bars, I do remember him telling me that if I ever went to prison in Louisiana someday, they didn't have air conditioning, so I should try to find a bunk by a fan.

He must've recognized the path I was on. I just thought what he said was some crazy almanac information to show how smart he was.

What made Dave "crazy" was that he was a brawler, a rough-cut guy who was not afraid to get into fistfights. He was fearless, but in a stupid sort of way. As summer turned to fall, Tammy and I got high and drunk, and as we ate Ecstasy with Dave, we talked about how much we loved each other (the drug will make you feel like you love everybody) when the truth was having him in the mix was becoming disruptive. He'd do his own stuff, but he was with us a lot because he didn't have a car, and he inevitably became a tagalong. We couldn't get rid of him, and we were starting to get a little afraid of him.

One night in December, Dave took my car, went out to a little bar right off the water, got drunk, and wrecked it. I think he drove it into the bayou. I never saw my car again after that.

Suddenly, I didn't have a vehicle—and Tammy and I decided we were tired of Crazy Dave. But the only way we were going to get away from him was by moving away, far away—and that meant returning to Dallas. All things considered, it sounded like an awfully good idea.

It wasn't.

In January, Tammy and I hit the road in her car, headed northwest, and got an apartment about 20 minutes from where my mom and My Ma lived. I found a job at a boat repair dealer, putting to work some of the skills I'd learned at the boatyard. I quickly hooked back up with the friends I had grown up with, the same ones I was with when I missed Christmas lunch all those years back, and they were all strung out doing and selling cocaine.

It was then that I really started snorting daily. I even did it in the bathroom at work. No wonder I only had that job for a month.

From then on, things went downhill fast.

Instead of buying a tiny bit here or an eight ball (one eighths of an ounce) there, I purchased several ounces of coke so that, as customers bought it from me, they wouldn't have to go anywhere else to get more to use or sell. I became a one-stop shop. Selling cocaine was a whole lot different than selling weed. With marijuana, someone can buy it and it'll last for a week, maybe longer. But cocaine customers used or sold their supply faster because they're snorting it, smoking it, and shooting it. It didn't matter how much they got. It never lasted, for me or for them.

Tammy and I stayed in the apartment for a few months, and I progressed from snorting cocaine to smoking it. My nose was so messed up from all the snorting. Smoking coke changed everything. Both have an intense high, but when you smoke it, you go from zero to a hundred in a matter of seconds, and you come down a whole lot faster, too. When you snort cocaine, you don't get the pure form of the drug. But when you smoke coke, you cook off all the impurities, so when it hits your system, it's much more potent.

Yet I knew the escalation of my cocaine use was not good. I could see what it was doing to everyone else.

~~~

One April day, I was at the apartment, and one of my friends was cooking up some crack in our bathroom. I looked at myself in the mirror and said quietly, "I know where this road leads."

I actually had no idea at all, but I thought I did.

I just jumped right on it, though, and I stayed on it.

Little did I know what was coming.

Not long after that, Tammy and I moved out of the apartment and rented a house closer to the where my mom lived. We got into a wreck in her car. I was backing up and either hit a tree or another vehicle, I was so high I don't recall for sure. The result, though, was we had no car because she could only afford comprehensive insurance. That made it harder to do my drug deals around town. Still, I was selling a lot of cocaine, but not enough to keep me in my habit.

In no time, everything got so out of control that we were out of the house and into a motel. There was a lot of drug activity there, and we got two rooms—one for sleeping, the other for doing and selling drugs. One night in July, I was in the bathroom smoking coke when I heard a knock on the door.

We had a secret knock, and it wasn't the correct cadence, but I opened the door anyway.

Slam! In came a bunch of cops. It was out of nowhere, and when they came in, it was almost like I was floating above it all, watching a scene from a movie. Emotionally, all I could think was, *What the hell just happened?* They searched the room, and I had drugs on me. They then announced they were going into the second room, the one where we slept. Tammy and another person were in there, but they had no drugs on them. After searching that room, the officers returned and cuffed me.

Something happened in my spirit the second they put those handcuffs on me. It was an undeniable sense that my freedom was gone. Crazy thing was, I already knew I wasn't free, that I was no longer in control of my life. But when those metal rings clicked around my wrists, it was as if I was being led down the road by a ring in my nose and that I'd already been sentenced.

The cuffs made it real. It was done.

That was my first drug-related arrest.

I was 18.

In jail, I was so malnourished from the cocaine use that the little bitty pot pies they provided at mealtime were not enough to quell my voracious hunger. I ate toilet paper just to put something in my stomach.

I was interrogated often, but I didn't give up any useful information. After four days, I finally got up the nerve to call my dad to tell him I had been arrested and the price of my bond: a cool 10 grand.

My father asked point blank, "Have you learned anything?"

"Well, the pot pies in jail are really small," I replied.

I wasn't being a smart ass. It was just the first thing that hit my mind.

He hung up the phone.

Clearly, I hadn't learned anything. Not what I should've, anyway.

A couple of days later I was released on my own recognizance, meaning the authorities trusted I'd show up for my court date.

I did, and it got postponed.

By the time the rescheduled date came, it wouldn't matter. I'd already be back in custody—because what I didn't realize as I left the jail was that the police were in the process of setting me up.

~~~~

I begged my mother and My Ma to let Tammy and I come and live with them. They did—and for the briefest time, I tried to actually behave like I *had* learned something. Even though I didn't have a vehicle, I got a job at Burger King. I tried to save money and get back on track. For a couple of months, I rarely used cocaine. I mainly smoked pot.

Then a couple of people started coming to me to get some deals done, and I accommodated them. They were small scores, nothing more. But one of the buyers had gotten himself in trouble with the law, and the undercover narcotics department was going to make sure I'd be the bait to get him out of trouble.

The initial transaction was an eight ball of cocaine. I sold it directly to a guy named Steve Smith. He was driving a pretty Porsche. He was also a cop. A couple of weeks later, he asked for a larger amount, an ounce, and I happily obliged. I'd later discover the escalating amounts were intentional, designed to get me to trust Steve so that when he asked for the big one, I'd sell to him without hesitation.

In September, he asked for a half kilo of cocaine, and I arranged, with four other people, to make the purchase on a Thursday evening at an apartment complex in Dallas. While I had never used the location before, I wasn't really worried about it—but one of the guys, Pierre, certainly was. As we awaited the exchange inside one of the units, he was pacing and rubbing his face.

"Man, something just doesn't feel right," he said.

"Oh, no, man," I reassured him. "Everything's fine."

"No," he insisted. "There's just a lot of traffic going on." He must've seen through the window there was more than the usual amount of activity going on outdoors.

Pierre walked outside, and when he didn't return after a few minutes, I stepped out and walked down the stairs.

Suddenly, something moved off to my right. My eyes darted in that direction to see someone jumping the little four-foot-high metal fence that cordoned off the swimming pool area—and he was coming right at me at a full run.

The person wasn't in uniform, so I didn't think it was a cop. *Perhaps it is another dopehead wanting to rob us.*

I took off, running as fast as I could. I was a little, bitty guy, no more than 120 pounds soaking wet, and I hoped my size would equate to speed. I sprinted down corridors between the apartment units and slashed through breeze-ways. I didn't have an escape route in mind as I ran. All I knew was I had to get away. Fast.

I dashed out across the parking lot to scale the wooden fence that separated the complex from the parking lot. As I landed, got my legs, and bolted forward, my pursuer appeared from a walkway to the side.

I saw a gun.

"Freeze! Get on the ground!"

I didn't do either, and as I tried to dodge past, he hit me in the face with his pistol.

Pain, pure and exquisite, seared through my head, and I nosedived onto the pavement.

I felt the man slam down with all his weight onto my back.

"I'll blow your f***ing head off!" he screamed as he wrestled to pull my arms behind my waist.

I felt blows to my stomach and my side. Others had arrived, and they were kicking me into submission.

Only when I was handcuffed and pulled off the ground and onto my feet did I see the gold badge on one of my assailants. *Cops.*

Horrified, I looked down at the blood splattering my tank top. Nobody had ever identified themselves as police officers, but my whirling mind started to put it all together despite my throbbing skull. *The fella who jumped at me from the swimming pool area must've been a plainclothes cop. They must've got Pierre before I came out of the apartment.*

The whole damn thing was a set up!

That was confirmed when I was forced over to the paddy wagon and saw Pierre and the others. Every one of the plain clothes officers began taunting us about the arrest and everything that led up to it. "Thanks for all the information. We really appreciate it," they jeered. "You guys knew this was a sting, didn't you?"

Then Steve Smith appeared around the corner of the vehicle, and all was crystal clear.

Not only had the deal been a set up, but *I* was the one who had been set up from the very beginning.

We were tossed into the back of the paddy wagon, which was essentially a little jail cell on wheels. As we felt the rumble of the vehicle pulling away from the apartment complex, one of the fellas spoke up.

"I still got some cocaine on me."

"We better do it," I replied—and we did, right there in the back of the wagon. He had the coke stuffed in his pants and socks, and we twisted and contorted in every which way to get the drug out and onto the black, vinyl bench seats, all while our hands and arms were cuffed behind our backs.

We must've looked ridiculous, on our knees with our heads bobbing down to snort up the cocaine as fast as we could. But we were addicts, and we had to get rid of any further evidence, right?

By the time we got to the jail in downtown Dallas, we were all high as kites. I was also coughing up blood from the abuse I took from the cops. I saw it as that, too. Abuse. It's not like I pulled a gun on any of them. I didn't even have one. I was just evading arrest, that's all. Did that really justify getting the crap beat out of me?

The paddy wagon came to a stop at the rear entrance of the jail, which was outdoors but under cover, like a parking garage but with a high ceiling and dingy, yellow lighting.

When I stepped down from the vehicle, my head grew heavy and my sight grew dim. Dizzy, I jerked my leg outward to keep from falling. I was scared, I honestly thought I could be hemorrhaging internally, and I was thinking to myself, *If I can get them to let me go to the hospital, maybe I can escape while I'm there.*

I finally convinced the authorities to take me to the hospital, but when I got there, I found out two things: one, I wasn't hemorrhaging, and two, I wasn't escaping. I was handcuffed to the bed. There was an officer with me the whole time. I wasn't going anywhere.

I was there for about two hours before I was returned to the jail at about 11 o'clock at night. I was taken straight to the holding tank. Emblazoned with harsh fluorescent light, it was at least 30 feet wide and 100 yards long, and it had a bunch of individual cells off the sides that went from one end to the other. Concrete and stainless steel benches peppered the perimeter, and there were easily 300 people lying together on, below, and between the benches and throughout the space, their heads resting on rolls of toilet paper. The combined body heat from everyone did nothing to diminish the chill of the room. It was freezing.

The tank reeked of piss, puke, and feces. Itty, bitty bathrooms were off the back wall, but it was so nasty I was afraid to go into one of them.

I ended up staying there, with no change of clothes and no shower, for two long days and nights as I was processed. The blood on my tank top became crusty and gave off a musty, metallic smell. We were fed sandwiches with paper-thin bologna and a racing stripe of mustard on the bread. At one point, I made a collect call to My Ma's house and spoke to her, my mother, and Tammy. I told them I needed them to get me out, but I didn't yet have my bond set. It was eventually set at $250,000, which meant I was in for the long haul.

Saturday morning, I was transferred to a cell in one of the oldest of the four county jails in Dallas, The Government

Center. When I arrived, I was put into an orange jumpsuit and given a mattress, towel, toothbrush and toothpaste, and a little thin bar of homemade lye soap. I was cuffed again, hands in front of me, so I could hug the mattress and other supplies to my body. After that, I was escorted by a guard and waddled forward down a main hallway, though a big iron door, and into a smaller area reminiscent of a shark cage. Before going into the cage, I was told to turn around and place my hands through a hole in the door I'd just passed through, and I was released from my handcuffs. The guard who escorted me stayed behind the iron door, leaving me in the cage alone.

I turned back around, and another door was electronically opened in front of me—to reveal a line of two four-man cells, all overcrowded with inmates.

One black head popped up and peeked through the bars. Then another, and another, and another, all the way down.

Holy crap! I thought, my heart pounding. *What in the world? I am in the wrong place.*

I wrapped my arm around a bar in the shark cage, and I was gripping it for dear life, as if I was hanging off the landing slide of an out-of-control helicopter.

"You gotta go in there," the guard told me from behind the door.

"I ain't going in there!" I tried to put some steel behind my trembling voice.

"Man, you gotta go in there."

"Listen!" I insisted. "I ain't going in there. I am in the wrong spot."

The guard saw I was scared. "Alright. Let me check this. Hold on."

He didn't have to tell me to do that. I snaked my arm around the bar and clung to it as he checked the papers attached to the clipboard he was carrying.

"Yep. There's been a mistake," he announced. "This is an all-black cell for aggravated offenders. Let's get you where you're supposed to be."

I'd never felt so relieved. *Phew, Lord Jesus!* It wasn't a racial thing. Most of the people I dealt with in the drug game, such as Pierre, were black. But I was terrified of what all those heavy hitters might've done to a little white guy like me.

As I was re-cuffed, someone behind me yelled out, "C'mon back here!"

I had to. I had left my mattress behind. I retrieved it as quickly as I could, and then I got myself out of there.

When we got to the next block, I still had a little trepidation, but as I stepped out of that area's shark cage and toward one of the cells, I could tell there was racial diversity and that quite a few of the inmates were older, even a bit frail.

It was less intimidating, but I was still on pins and needles as the guard pushed the button to open the door to let me go in.

The entire cell block was probably no more than 800 square feet, with two toilets and sinks and a pair of skinny three-foot-by-three-foot shower stalls to one side. On the other side was a barred area with the two cells, and each one of the four-man cells were about the size of a standard guest bedroom, perhaps a tad smaller. Mine was packed double its capacity, so it was pretty snug. The air was stale, the lighting was faint, and the bunk awaiting the mattress I carried was nothing more than a hard, steel shelf welded to the wall.

There was no privacy. It was so crowded someone could've farted and knocked me over, so I suppose my diminutiveness worked to my advantage. But that didn't make me feel any better.

I was frightened. My cellmates, whites and blacks and Hispanics, were street brothers, institutionalized dudes that had been locked up a long time, and those stories that you hear about what happens in prison *do* happen.

Man, I'm in a lot of trouble.

It was probably about six o'clock in the morning when I got there. I was exhausted, and I remember this older black man they called Pop asked if I wanted a cigarette. I wondered if it was a trap. I didn't even smoke at the time.

I took one, rolled up tobacco with no filter, and coughed it down to calm my nerves. Surprisingly, no one laughed at me. They knew I had never been in a prison like this before. It was that obvious.

~~~~

I was in that cell for nearly five months before I got sentenced. In that time, nothing bad was done to me. Perhaps that was because the guards did a patrol every 30 minutes or so to make sure everybody was doing what they were supposed to do, and the one guard who originally put me in the wrong shark cage, a young guy in his twenties, kept his eye on me. I think he recalled how scared I was. Maybe I wasn't harmed because my fellow prisoners saw something of themselves in me. It could be that they were simply never in the mood for trouble. I don't know what spared me. I was just glad I got out of there unscathed.

I passed the time playing cards and dominoes, telling a bunch of lies, and watching TV. The TV was old (it looked like it had an actual picture tube), and it was positioned outside the cell, just close enough for one of us to reach through and change the channels. There weren't many of those to choose from, and the biggest controversy among the inmates was regarding what we were going to watch. This led to more than a few heated discussions, so I stayed out of it. I went along with whatever was on.

There was no exercise time. Breakfast, lunch, and dinner were served to us in our cells. We never left. I grabbed a shower whenever I could get one. There was a phone in the cell block that looked like a pay phone minus the coin slot, but it was so crowded and noisy it was impossible to have a private conversation. I talked to my dad every week or so. He hired an attorney for me that must've cost him a fortune, and I was living on a pipe dream, trying to convince myself I was going to get out of trouble and not go to prison because it was my first offense. I called My Ma's, too, and spoke to her or mom or Tammy, but communication with them tapered off while I was incarcerated. Mom remained very sick then, too.

Mark went to school in the downtown area near the jail and visited a few times, usually in the evening. He once smuggled in some Xanax and joints, passing the contraband through a straw that we poked through the keyhole in the area where the phones were located. We'd be taken to a holding tank behind a steel wall to get to where the little booths were located. They were much like the ones I'd seen on television, with a corded phone on each side of a window, except that the window in these booths was tiny by comparison, about the size of a person's face. Mom and My Ma stopped by, too, when they could, but they didn't smuggle anything in. Those visits were brief, about 20 minutes each. It was a lot for my family to come all the way into downtown Dallas. They usually had to take the bus.

I didn't have a lot to talk about other than wanting to get out of jail. My life wasn't worth crap, so I didn't have anything to contribute to the conversation. They tried to be supportive and encouraging, and I was more than glad to see them. It was like getting a drink of water in the desert. Having a visitor, in fact, was the only time we got out of our cells.

Finally, the day of my sentencing arrived. I spent the better part of an entire day in a cell in the courthouse before being taken into the courtroom. Mom, my brother, My Ma, and Tammy were all in attendance. My father and everyone else in Louisiana couldn't make the trip.

Despite what I assume were the best efforts of my father's attorney (I may have met with him once, I really don't remember), the judge threw the book at me. The assistant district attorney prosecuting the case told the court, "Yeah, your honor, he was moving up awfully fast in the drug world. He first got an eight ball of cocaine followed up by an ounce followed by a half kilo. We recommend 30 years."

The judge's confirmation followed: a 10-year sentence for each of the three drug charges running concurrently. *Did I just get 30 years?* I thought to myself as I was being led from the courtroom. *I don't even know what 'concurrent' means.* Once I was back at my cell, I was able to call my mother and she explained it: I'd be serving all three 10-year sentences at the same time.

That was it.

I was going to prison. The real thing—and, apparently, for a very long time.

~~~~~

I was transferred out of the county jail within the next week—but right before I left, my mom came by to visit. Since I knew I was going to have my head shaved when I got to prison, I gave myself a buzz cut. When I saw mother through the tiny window, I was so happy to see her, and she was doing her very best to cheer me up. She had a smile on her face, but despite the little girl pigtails in her hair that she normally didn't wear, she looked old.

Tired. I could see the jaundice in her eyes. Mom was so sick.

But her physical weakness didn't negate her sense of humor.

"You look like a bald onion," she told me.

It was quite the ice breaker to what ended up being a very emotional meeting. I know my mom was scared for me, and I tried to be brave so she wouldn't be afraid. I was the first person from our family to ever be in this situation. At 18 years old, I was far from a grown man. At that moment, I knew I was as dumb and immature as I could possibly be. *Here I am, her baby boy, and she has to see me like this.* I wanted to cry.

At the end of our time together, my mom prayed for my protection. "Abba Father," (she always called God, "Abba"), "protect Doug right now. Send your angels to guard him and keep him safe. Help my son to know you love him and are with him."

There was no doubt she had a special relationship with the Lord. Ever since I could remember, mom had a hard-back, olive-green edition of The Living Bible. It seemed like it was eight inches thick, and it was marked up with pen, colored up with highlighters, filled with notes, and it contained poems she wrote to God.

Mom definitely struggled. She couldn't get out of her own bondage to alcohol.

But, man, she loved the Lord.

I was taken to a prison where I'd be processed for a week before being relocated to my permanent destination. Though I understood it wasn't where I was going to stay for good, the ride there on the Bluebird bus in the wee hours of the morning was awful. My feet were shackled, I had waist chains on, and my hands were cuffed in front of my body. I jangled to my seat, and then I was fastened to it. It was dark outside, nothing to see in the gloom, and the ride was long and bumpy.

I prayed that wherever I was going to end up would somehow, someway, be safe for me. I had no clue what to expect. The previous five months in jail had made me no braver, that was for sure.

As we pulled up to the processing prison, I took in the triple fences, razor wire, and armed guards everywhere. My heart sank. I was assigned to another cell and pretty much slept with one eye open the entire time I was there. "Whatever you do, don't sleep with your head on the end of the bed where the bars are," one inmate had told me. "They just might cut your throat."

If that's how it is here, I wondered, *how bad is it going to be at the next place?*

That next place was Hilltop, a medium-security prison for first offenders in Gatesville, Texas. It was named for its location atop one of the highest points in the region, not that

I ever got to enjoy whatever view that afforded. As I was first brought in and processed, I was strip searched—again. I don't know how many times someone can be strip searched in the custody of the department of corrections. It seemed like every time I turned around, I was baring my butt checks and lifting my sac for someone. But they were basically pissing on their tree, doing anything they could to humiliate you, letting you know they were in charge, and making you feel a little less human.

From there, I was taken with the other newbies (the other inmates called us "fresh fish") and paraded around camp like some new wild animal being brought into the zoo. They took us out of this place and into that place, and everywhere we went I felt like there were 800 eyes staring me down, checking me out, and sizing me up. I could only imagine what they were thinking about me.

Small, thin, scared little boy.

It was late afternoon by the time I was taken to my cell—which, in this case, was inside a dormitory-style space with each personal area in a cell feeling more like an office cubicle. Nothing was more than waist high in and around the tiny five-by-seven foot space. I had a bunk, a little metal locker below the bunk, and a small writing table attached to it. These cubicles were in one, huge room, with block walls partitioning off the showers and toilets. I counted out about 40 of us sharing the room, and my fellow inmates were fairly young. They appeared to be anywhere from 18 to 32 years old. It was a diverse group: blacks, whites, and Hispanics. Everybody segregated themselves by their race, which was not what I'd seen at the jails before and was not at all how I grew up.

I recalled all the stories I knew about prison gangs and having to possibly pick a side, and all of my worst fears from things I'd seen on TV about survival behind bars rose to the surface. "Don't ever be scared if you have to get into a fight," echoed in my mind from something I'd heard. "If you get beat up, and you don't fight back, everybody will run over you."

My stomach roiled. *I'm gonna have to figure this out.*

In the chow hall, we were split into two lines. We couldn't talk or ask for anything. I put my tray out, they slung the food on there, and I sat down where I was told to sit. There was a special prison etiquette to follow, things you do and don't do such as reach across somebody else's plate. Problem was that first night I hadn't been there long enough to know what those rules were. I filled it in as I went. I remember making some small talk to the fella eating next to me, but I didn't know who was who. I do recall that I learned to quit liking food in prison. It was nasty.

After dinner, we were returned to our dormitory area and counted along the way. They were always counting us to make sure everyone was there. The TV was on, and I tried to keep to myself—but one surprising thing I discovered about prison was that good always came out in the people you were with. They were willing to help out, lend you something, ask if you needed anything, and several people came around and introduced themselves. They were nosy, trying to find out information, but they were also kind.

I didn't expect that, and it made me feel a little less on edge.

Still, I did not have a restful night. It was me and 40 other people. Inmates. Hardened guys.

A pretty long day turned into an awfully long night as I tried to anticipate what was ahead.

~~~~~

Right away, I learned how to do the Texas Two-Step. Every day, I was taken outside the prison on the work line in big, dirt fields along the nearby highway. A bunch of gun-toting guards stood by as we chopped away at chest-high weeds and grass with a hoe that felt like it weighed a good 20 pounds. Up went the hoe and down it came, and we shuffled forward.

One, two step. One, two step. Sometimes we even did the four step.

It was excruciating work, broken only when a huge water truck came by to give us a drink and a chance to have a cigarette. "Smoke 'em if you've got 'em!" the guards hollered. We were returned, strip searched, and led to the prison chow hall for lunch, only to be returned in the afternoon for another shift in the fields before yet another strip search when we got back to the prison.

That's what I did Monday-Friday for the first three months. If someone got in trouble, they ended up scrubbing bricks back at the prison for 12 straight hours. I ended up doing that a couple of times. I had a big mouth, and sometimes it got me in trouble. We were given rec time every day, but we were back in our cells every night after dinner.

Eventually, I was given an assignment off the work line. I took a job in the kitchen where I ultimately became a clerk because I could type well enough. That's what I did the next four months or so.

Until I was released.

Yep. Those three, 10-year terms served concurrently actually translated to just over a year behind bars, including the time I spent in the county jail. At the time, Texas was so overcrowded in their prisons and jails, they had a "good time" law in effect that stated inmates had to serve one-quarter of a sentence. They gave us 45 days "good time" for every 30 days served.

Too short? A slap on the wrist? Maybe. But I came out of that brief time in prison worse off than I went in. I ended up diving into the violence of prison culture. I wasn't the biggest guy when I got there, but I hit a growth spurt and put on a lot of size. When I got out, Mark told me my body had gotten too big for my head. But I was 19, and I guess I felt like I had something to prove.

One time we were going through the serving line for breakfast, and there was the one guy with whom I just didn't get along. As I got my tray, he took a spatula with no food on it and slammed it down on top of my tray. He made some comment to me, I made some comment to him, and then I kept going through the line to get my grub. I tried not to pay any attention to him. Later, as I bent down to put my tray into the serving area, he sucker-punched me right in the face. We got into a fight right there and then.

While I didn't instigate that one, I did start other incidents throughout my stay. Beyond that, I didn't try to join a gang or anything like that. It's not that there wasn't opportunity to do so. I just avoided it.

It was also at Hilltop where I first started reading the Bible again. I didn't know enough about it to recognize the Old Testament from the New, but as I randomly read, there was stuff I remembered from when I was growing up and going to church, and somehow, it was more real to me.

It wasn't enough to change me, but it did make an impression.

How much of one I wasn't going to find out until much later.

First, I still had some rough living to do and lessons to learn.

CHAPTER THREE

———

STUCK ON STUPID

ON MY FIRST DAY OF FREEDOM, I hit the ground running.

I got drunk and slept with my friend's wife's sister.

It was weird how it all came about. It started with a fella I met while in prison who was a couple of years older than me, though our birthdays were just days apart. We ended up becoming really good friends despite the fact that he was a thief.

Oddly, I have little tolerance for people who steal. I'm not sure where the peeve came from. I guess I believe that if someone works hard for something and then has it taken away from them, there's no work ethic in that. A lot of my fights in prison were with inmates who had stolen something from other prisoners. Yet I got along with this guy, who was actually behind bars for a burglary conviction, just fine.

Anyway, his wife and her sister visited him often because they lived about 45 minutes from the prison, and over time, his sister-in-law paid me a couple of visits as well. It was nice to have the company. No one from my family was really close enough to visit regularly, and I hadn't heard anything from Tammy since my incarceration had begun. I wrote her, or other family members often, but usually no one wrote back. Plus, we weren't able to use the phone in prison like we could at the county jail. In fact, we were allowed only one call every 90 days, assuming you didn't get written up for anything, and I'd had more than my share of write ups for fighting.

It was eventually through a letter from Mark that I learned Tammy had left and gone back to her family in Mississippi. It's not like we officially broke up or anything, but it was like getting a Dear John letter without the Dear John part.

So, my friend's wife's sister became a good distraction. I suppose she might have even been pretty.

When it was time for my release, my prison buddy offered to let me have his car, a red 1976 Chevy Camaro that ended up sounding a whole lot cooler than it actually was. Still, it was wheels, and I was going to need them, whether I headed up to Dallas or back down to Louisiana.

On September 9, 1990, prison officials transported me and five other released prisoners by cab to Killeen, Texas, where we were then left on our own wearing the clothes on our back (prison issue shoes, pants, and a shirt that didn't fit) and $200 cash. My friend's wife and her sister met me there in the Camaro, and on the way to their place they took me to a store to buy a pair of pants, socks, underwear, and a shirt, and then we went elsewhere to get a six pack of Coronas.

When we got back to their place, we got something to eat, and I downed five beers. The sister and I then headed off to her bedroom, and one thing led to another. I probably talked her into doing something she didn't want to do, but since she took her pants down and got naked, I suppose she wanted to do it, too.

I didn't really like her, though. I never had. I just wanted sex.

The next morning, I got up, got my stuff and the keys to the Camaro, and headed toward Dallas. The car sputtered along. The steering column was broken, but it got me there, even through the heavy freeway traffic. I hadn't called anyone to tell them I'd been released, much less that I was coming into town. So, when I pulled up to My Ma's house and walked up to the door at 9:45 that morning, it was a complete surprise.

My Ma was so glad to see me she whipped up three eggs over easy with toast, bacon, and grits. Man, nothing had ever tasted so good. I was high on the hog.

Now, to get high again on something else.

I headed out and tracked down Danny, one of the drug buddies I used to hang out with when I first did cocaine. It was great. We drove around smoking a big 'ol fat joint. Later, we went downtown and picked up Mark from school, again a total surprise. Then the three of us went and smoked more dope.

The second day of freedom never smelled so good—or familiar.

Eventually, we dropped Danny off at his place and headed to Baylor University Medical Center. That's where mom was hospitalized, and had been, I understood, for quite some time. The only call I was allowed while I was in prison was an emergency call to my grandmother's house after receiving a letter from my mom. My brother had answered the phone when I called, confirming what the letter had said: that mom was so sick she was in the hospital and close to death.

I just had to see her.

When I walked into the room, she saw me and cried tears of joy. I didn't like what I saw, though. She looked really emaciated. I have small hands, but her wrists were so small I could circle my thumb and my middle finger all the way around one of them. She also had bedsores. Baylor was a great hospital, and maybe she was just too embarrassed or weak to ask for help, but at that moment, it broke my heart. I called for the nurse through the buzzer, and when she came in, I lit into her.

"Here is my mom. She can't even take care of herself, and y'all aren't even keeping her from getting bedsores on her butt, or cleaning and taking care of her!" I was mad, and

I told them I was going to come back every day. "When I do, I better not see this."

Of course, I was feeling pretty guilty, too. There I was, stoned out of my mind, while my mom was laying there, suffering from liver disease.

I did come back every day, and the care did get better. I had missed my mom, wondering whether she was going to live or die.

She finally got her transplant a couple of weeks after my release.

I ended up staying with My Ma and Mark for a couple of days, and I finally got around to checking in with my parole officer, before asking my sister, Penny, if I could crash with her for a while. She was no longer dancing and had, in fact, settled down with a boyfriend named Ken. He was a musician, but not your typical sort. He didn't drink or do drugs. Penny smoked some pot with me now and again over the next couple of weeks, all behind his back.

It was clear Ken didn't like me much, and the feeling was mutual. He was verbally abusive to my sister, and one night, after I heard the two of them getting carried away in a shouting match, I told him a few choice things, followed by a threat.

"If you ever touch my sister, I'm gonna kill you!"

"You need to get the hell out of here!" he told me.

"Fine. I will," I responded, "but don't make me come back."

From there I went to My Ma's for the next week. I had no where else to go at the moment. Mom had just been released from the hospital after her transplant, so going there allowed me to see her. It was good to have her home. I'd love to say that I was the good son who stayed at her bedside, catering to her every need and telling her jokes, but I didn't do any of that. I just checked in on her. The first couple of months, mom took medication to make sure her body didn't reject the new liver. We were still unsure. She was out of the woods, but it was a long way from being okay. Mom was still pale and pasty, but the yellow jaundice was gone, and her eyes were starting to clear up.

No matter what, mom was always silly and corny. She kept a smile on her face to hide how she was really feeling. "You've just got to keep on trucking." That what she always said. But we knew her well enough to know she was downplaying the pain, and we went along with her silliness.

With everything so up in the air, I thought it might be a good time to visit my father. I had called my dad the day I returned to Dallas after getting out of prison. Once I returned to My Ma's from Penny's, I contacted him again, and he thought I should head down to see him. My father had this thing about going camping anytime he thought we should talk. He told me we needed to get the tent, go out into the woods, and spend some time together.

I drove there in the rickety red Camaro, and we went to a place our family had gone many times before, to Percy Quin State Park about 90 minutes from Slidell near McComb, Mississippi. We camped at the same spot about 40 yards down the hill into the woods towards the edge of Lake Tangipahoa. It was a remote place away from the showering areas and parking spots where other park visitors hooked up their mobile homes or RVs.

It was dense with loblolly pines and magnolia trees, and seasonal flowers peppered the area with their bright colors and sweet aromas. To be out there again in the wilderness was light years away from the dorm and the razor wire of prison. We rarely got to go outside when it was dark while I was incarcerated, and whenever we did, all I did was look up at the night sky. Being at the campsite with the moon and the stars and the water was something I just had to take in.

God's world is so different at night. Having freedom like that tasted wonderful. It makes an impact to lose something and have it given back to you—but I was still such an idiot. As much as I thought it was great, I trampled on it by continuing to do the things I wasn't supposed to do.

I wasn't taking freedom seriously.

Dad and I stayed out there for a couple of days and nights. We took my dad's old yellow boat out onto the lake. It was a 16-footer with an outboard motor, and I had often driven it from the cockpit when we went water skiing on family camping trips. Dad and I went fishing, but since we always did catch and release, we brought in food like hot dogs or hamburgers to cook up for our meals instead of fish. We lit up the Coleman lanterns at night and built a big fire kindled from wood gathered around the spot, hoping the smoke would keep the mosquitos at bay.

My dad and I had always been close. I was the firstborn boy, the one who always wanted to be with him the most. It was nice, just the two of us. It was the first time I'd ever been camping alone with him, and despite the circumstances, it wasn't weird. It was a grown-up camping trip, even if I wasn't really a grown up at all.

We did a lot of talking, of course. He asked questions like, "What are your plans?" "What did you think about when you were in prison?" "How do you want your life to be different?" My dad was a psychologist, and I was always good about giving the right answers. I told him I wanted to find a good job and enroll in college. Work ethic was never a problem. I'd always been a hard worker. I knew how to get by.

I didn't just give him wishful answers or try to lie my way through some of my responses. I was being honest. It was really what I wanted to do and be, but I simply didn't have the maturity to actually carry it out. I was still pretty stupid.

Not my dad. He was a smart man. He was trying to find out if I had really changed at all while I was behind bars— and he rightly concluded that I hadn't.

"You haven't learned much," he told me, "and prison has really rubbed off on you. You act like you are still in prison. You talk like you are still in prison."

His words didn't make me angry. I knew I was just as dumb as the day before I went to jail, maybe dumber.

After dad and I returned from camping, I spent a few more days with everyone. It was nice to see Aimee, and the visit ended on a good note when I made another shopping trip with my stepmom, Christine. We talked and reconnected. Instead of asking questions, she tried to help me see the answers. With my dad it was, "What's your plan?" With her it was, "Let's talk about how you get there." She was the only person who had ever communicated with me that way.

~~~~~

Before heading home, I also went to Mississippi to see Tammy where she was living with her parents. When I showed up, she answered the door and invited me in. I said hello and greeted everyone, then we went outside and sat on the front porch. I still had feelings for her, but they were faint and fleeting, connected only to the past. "You let me down," I said, "but I messed you over, so I guess I am the one that needs to be apologizing."

There was no hug or kiss. I just wanted to tell her I was sorry.

We then went back inside, and I apologized to her family. They had really liked me. I was raised to use manners and say, "Yes, sir," and "No, sir." I was polite and cordial. I guess maybe they saw something in me.

I was a messed up individual, but I suppose I was a good messed up individual.

I never saw Tammy again after that. I didn't even properly tell her goodbye.

I drove back to Dallas on a Sunday night. I'd traveled about eight hours and was only 20 minutes from home when I was pulled over on Highway 80 in Forney, Texas and got tickets for speeding, expired tags, not having a driver's license, not wearing a seatbelt, and for not having car insurance, all at one time, to the tune of about $500 I didn't have. He also gave me a warning about having an expired inspection on the vehicle.

I had about a quarter of an ounce of weed in the car, but the trooper didn't find it. I stashed it under the passenger side carpet on the floorboard when the trooper went to the first car he pulled over that was right in front of me. It was a good thing he stopped both of us, or I wouldn't have had time to hide the marijuana. He never searched the car. It was a miracle I didn't get arrested.

Back in Dallas, I continued the apartment search I had started before heading south, and I found one at the beginning of November. I had sold enough marijuana to pay for the deposit and first month's rent. In no time, I had returned to my old, dopehead ways, minus the cocaine. I wasn't selling or doing coke anymore.

Before Christmas, I got a job at a bowling alley. I was a customer service attendant, a needlessly fancy name for someone who cleaned tables, picked up trash, threw away beer bottles, and made sure the bowling balls were where they were supposed to be. Janitor was far more accurate. I was making minimum wage, about $3.80 an hour, enough money to buy some cigarettes and a pack of gum, but certainly not enough to stop me from dealing weed.

Not that I would've stopped anyway. Even the tainted drug screens I turned in to my parole officer didn't prevent me from selling and using.

I was 19, dealing weed, getting dirty screens but still beating the rap, and I even had a couple of girls on the side.

I thought everything revolved around me. I was king of the world.

Funny thing how kingdoms tend to fall.

~~~~~

Two big things happened in 1991. First, I met a woman at the bowling alley. She worked at the bar, and she was about six years older than me. It started out like any other relationship I'd had before. We hung out and got to know one another. She had her own place, and we started having sex, but I wasn't being all that cautious. I was still seeing another girl, too, but I didn't care. I'm ashamed of my behavior now, but back then, in all honesty, my relationship with her was an escape from my way of life. I didn't have anything other than selling my weed and working my little job. I had never dated someone who was mature and responsible before. I didn't know what I was doing.

Then she called me one day and said she wanted to talk. She picked me up from my apartment. We went for what was a mostly silent and longer-than-usual ride before she blurted it out just as we rounded the corner back to my place.

"I'm pregnant."

I couldn't believe my ears. I was so selfish. I really did not want a kid then. I was still a kid myself. My life was screwed up. I wasn't smart enough to see it from that perspective at that moment, but the truth was, I did not want to have a kid that would have some of the same experiences I had, much less do the same things I was doing. I had been to prison. I was twisted and into drugs and partying.

It was never a case of the child being unwanted. I just wasn't ready to be a father, especially if I was going to be responsible to some extent to raise the child—and I didn't want to bring a child into the world that would face the same things I had.

Today, I have a relationship with that child, a daughter, and I am very grateful for the relationship I have with her and with my grandchildren.

As for her mother and I, there are definitely two versions of every story, and mine is probably the one that is wrong. For the most part, we remained cordial. I felt like she left the door open for me to be part of her life, but I was so messed up and self-centered, I didn't know what I wanted, so I just ran from everything. She lived the life she had without me, and I lived the life I had without her.

There was very little communication between us during the pregnancy. The day she gave birth to our daughter, I got a call from her saying she was at the hospital and had just had the baby, but when I asked her which hospital, she said she'd call me back. She didn't call again until she was home with the infant.

Her mother did let me help pick our daughter's name. For that, I am also grateful.

Second, that same year, my mother returned to drinking. The giveaway was the way she carried around a cup with a lid and a straw, so no one could really smell what was in it. She also severely watered down her alcohol, but we all knew. In addition, Dallas was a dry area then, but she made bus rides to go to the wet areas near the city to get her booze. Both were old behaviors renewed.

Members of the family confronted her a few times, me included, but my brother and I sometimes smoked pot with her, so telling her she didn't need to drink when we were lighting up was pretty much self-contradictory. An oxymoron from my moronic behavior.

Mom also went through a serious bout with depression, and it was understandable. She'd had the transplant. I was out on my own. My brother was about to finish school and move out, too. Life was changing for her big time. He and I visited when we could, but nothing was the same as before. Plus, her situation at home wasn't the best. She was living with My Ma, my uncle who was bipolar and had his manic moments all the time, and even my great-grandmother had joined them. She was in her nineties and had been brought there from Abilene to make sure she was safe.

It's no wonder mom got depressed and returned to the alcohol. It was simply too much.

I ended up getting a roommate at my apartment. His name was Tim, and he moved in with me after splitting up with his girlfriend. He was my downstairs neighbor. I met him one day when I was walking up the stairs. He had his door open and the music up loud, and I smelled some pot coming out of his place. I was like a moth drawn to the flame.

We became good friends as we learned we had both been in jail and prison before. We did drugs. We liked to party. He had the ability to get dope for me from connections that I didn't have, and I likewise had the ability to get dope for him. It usually came down to who could get the best stuff at the best price. Tim and I got closer, almost like brothers, as our loyalty to each other grew because of the lifestyle we were living. He became my first really close male friendship that wasn't from my family, and there were very few people we felt like we could trust outside of our inner circle. That was our safe spot.

But there was a problem. Tim was like Crazy Dave back in Louisiana—only Tim was the real thing. I wasn't selling cocaine or doing cocaine or meth, but Tim was. Not only that, he introduced me into the guns and violence. Back then, the Glock 9 and the mini Uzi were popular, but I never carried a gun. Carrying a firearm meant an automatic aggravated charge and immediate revocation of my parole, but on top of that, something just scared me about having a gun. Not Tim, though. He'd go out on the balcony of our apartment right off Interstate 635 in Dallas and fire off the Glock or the Uzi (sometimes both), even with all that traffic and congestion nearby.

Tim just didn't care. If he thought somebody had messed him over, he was the kind of guy that was going to go kick in the door and take back whatever had been taken from him. Tim was a kind person, but there was always that dark side that came out when he was doing drugs or when he felt somebody had played him. He wanted that tough guy reputation. His dad was a biker, so he grew up around that sort of thing.

Yet when Tim needed to kick in a door or make a threat, I didn't accompany him. I'd had my share of fights and stuff, don't get me wrong, but I'm not a violent person—at least not in the "shoot and get yourself killed" sort of way.

For the first time, I truly saw someone's life turned inside out by drug dealing and the life that goes with it. I got dragged along with it, too, in that people knew who he was, and because we ran together and lived together, I was guilty by association. I put myself in danger just because he was my roommate. I wasn't really scared of anyone—except Tim.

As it was getting really, really crazy with Tim, I met a girl at a club. Her name was Bethany, an athletic blonde and former gymnast who was in Dallas from Pittsburgh to visit family. We talked and exchanged numbers, and I found myself really taken by her. From her funny Pittsburgh accent (her "yinz" was the equivalent of a Texas "y'all") to her sense of responsibility and ambition, she was interesting, from another part of the country, and different from any girl I'd been with before.

Five years older than me, Bethany was smart, a college graduate with a degree in mass communications. Her attraction to me, I think, came down to the stereotypical good guy-bad guy type of thing that most of the girls I messed with seemed to like. They were fairly good girls who had a little bad side to them, and they were drawn to the good boy who was also the bad boy. Plus, I didn't like the kind of girls others usually associated with the dopehead part of me. No whores. No sluts. I despised topless dancers. I didn't want to mess with girls that were like me, or, at least, that aspect of me.

After meeting Bethany and starting a friendship with her, I began thinking more than ever about how I wanted to phase myself out of my old life. I was trying to do the right things, and while I still smoked and sold pot, the direction Tim was going with cocaine and meth was the same path that sent me to prison. All of it put a nasty taste in my mouth.

The proverbial icing on the cake came one morning in September when Tim showed up at the apartment after I hadn't seen him for about a week. He said he could score me a couple of pounds of weed (summers were a dry time of the year to find marijuana) if I gave him the money. We'd done that before, and I gave him the money—but I knew I'd been burned a couple of hours later after I didn't hear back from him. I never saw the drugs, and I decided it was time for me to go. When he ripped me off, the line had been crossed.

I got five people who didn't know Tim and who had five trucks, and we loaded up everything. I didn't tell anyone. I knew I had to secretly leave before I did something stupid or I got into a situation where I felt like I had to take a stand against him.

I later learned Tim destroyed the apartment when he found out what I had done. Better it than me.

Tim did catch up with me, though. My brother Mark was bringing me home from work one night when I saw Tim's car in the parking lot of the apartment complex where I'd moved to in Mesquite. How he found out where I lived, I don't know, but there he was.

"Make the block one more time," I instructed Mark. As he did, I took off my necklace, figuring that way Tim couldn't choke me with it. I thought, *This is going to be bad.*

We made the loop, and I told Mark to drop me off and leave. *No reason involving him in whatever's going to happen next.*

I walked straight up to Tim's car.

"Dude, what's up?" I asked, trying to sound as nonchalant as possible.

"Man, you moved out," Tim said, stating the obvious. "What's the deal?"

I responded, "Man, you ripped me off."

No, we weren't conversational geniuses, but it escalated until one of two things were going to happen. We'd either get into a fight over what he did to me or what he felt I did to him, or—well, I didn't know for sure.

"So," I finally ventured, "what do you want to do?"

Tim smiled. "Come on, man, let's go for a ride."

"I'm not going for a ride with you," I replied.

"What do you think I'm gonna do, kill you?"

I thought that was distinctly possible, but my pride being what it was, I certainly wasn't going to back down.

I got in the car. I was so nervous.

We ended up smoking a joint together. I guess it was our peace pipe—because after that, I hardly saw him again.

Not long after that, Tim killed himself. Rather, he killed the person who was in the car with him and then blew his head off.

Apparently, I got out while the getting was good.

~~~~~

One of the many negative consequences of my time with Tim was that I was fired from the bowling alley after he and I made a trip down to South Padre Island. A cop pulled us over as we were on our way there. He smelled weed, and I took the rap. I got arrested, and word must've reached my employer because I lost my job. I remained unemployed until I moved away from Tim and got the apartment in Mesquite.

That's when I hooked up with Joe, a fella I'd met while in prison. I went with him one day when he applied for a job at a tanning salon, and we gave them the phone number to my apartment to use as contact information. Joe was kind of flighty, so when the salon called several times to follow up with him, I had no idea where he was.

Finally, I made up an excuse. "Joe doesn't live here anymore. I haven't seen him in a while."

"Well, he interviewed for the job," the other person on the line said, "and we offered it to him. We just wanted to tell him he had the job if he wanted it."

I told them I didn't know how to get in touch with him.

"Do you want the job?" the person asked.

My parole officer had been on me to go back to work.

"Okay," I said. "I'll take it."

Just like that, in late 1991, I began working as a bed cleaner in a tanning salon.

By Christmas, I took in Bethany as my roommate. We'd stayed in touch over the phone, and I had even gone out east once to visit her and meet her family. Ironically, her father and brother were cops. I was the kind of guy they usually put in the back of the car. But, as I always could, I put on my best behavior in front of them, and they liked me. On that visit, I asked her to consider moving in with me. She had other family in Rockwall, part of the Dallas-Ft. Worth metroplex, and they believed there were job opportunities for her there in communications. She decided to move all the way from Pennsylvania to be with me.

Only then, after she moved in, did I consider her to be my girlfriend.

As 1992 got underway, I had a sense that my life was turning around for the better. At the tanning salon, one of the owners came into the store one day, saw me selling one of our products to a customer, and came up to me. I didn't know who he was, so I presented the product to him, and he was impressed. With his recommendation, I went through the organization's sales program, and in no time, I was promoted to assistant manager.

I was transferred to a store near north Dallas where I could work under one of their top salespeople, and I thrived. The salon had 21 different locations, and the stores were always in competition with each other. I came in as a nobody and won employee of the month or sales of the month for seven months in a row. I broke every sales record they had. I was a selling machine. I realized I had a gift, a natural talent, in sales. Bethany and I had even moved into a condominium near the store, so we'd live closer to work.

I had a good job and a steady girl. I was living in a condominium—and I had even stopped smoking pot. I was still selling it, though, and drinking Coronas like water.

But I *was* doing better.

I had even started taking some college classes. Before long, though, I was struggling to work full time and manage the rest of my life, so I called my dad to get some advice.

It was a Saturday in early October, and it was going to prove pivotal to deciding what I was going to do next.

"Why are you struggling?" dad asked.

"I'm trying to do school. I'm trying to do my job. I'm trying give each one 100 percent, but it's not working," I said. "I'm taking classes in the morning and classes at night, and I feel like I'm going from one place to another."

"Well, what do you want to do?"

It was just like when we were camping. He only asked open-ended questions.

"I want to give 100 percent at whatever I do. That has always been my thing."

My dad replied, "If work is too much and you need to work a little less to give 100 percent at school, we can help you out."

His mindset wasn't a surprise. He and Christine were professionals. To them, a college education should have been seen as my ticket.

It wasn't for me. I'd always had the intelligence and ability to get good grades, but sitting in a classroom for three hours on a Monday night listening to somebody talk about something that I didn't want to learn just didn't float my boat.

I was direct. "Dad," I said, "you can't afford my lifestyle." I had a condo. I was paying for my classes. I had a girlfriend, and we went out a lot to eat or have fun. I knew there was no way they could give me the money to support my bills and expenses. It wasn't like I was living high and mighty, but I had money on the side from selling pot.

"I just need to figure out how to keep doing what I am doing and living the way I am living," I concluded. "Doing less work and you helping me pay some bills is not gonna work."

We hung up, and I dropped out of school a few days later.

I was going to do more with my job—and I had a good idea how I was going to proceed.

~~~~~

Right after that conversation with my dad, I thought about Jerome. He was a sales colleague who worked at a different salon, but in the same company. He had been the king of the sales mountain at the franchise before I'd come in and dethroned him. I only saw him a few times a month at companywide sales meetings, but we reached out to each other by phone and developed a friendly relationship. He had ideas and dreams, and I had ideas and dreams. We discovered they lined up with each other, so we decided to merge our vision. We both figured our skill sets would work well with one another.

Jerome and I had been looking at different tanning salon purchasing options in the metroplex, and I was following his lead, but we'd never found an option that had enough customer volume or was in the right area.

I went to Bethany. "I need to go to Louisiana and try to find a tanning salon. The market in Dallas was very thick and saturated."

I doubt my declaration caught her by surprise. When I get focused on something, I'm just like a bulldog. She knew I was so determined that I was going to do it, no matter what.

"Where are you going to find one?" she asked.

"I don't know, but I will."

Monday morning, I called Jerome after our morning sales meeting. "I'm going to head to Louisiana around Christmastime and try to find us a salon."

"Christmas would be too late," Jerome replied. "That is right when the season is about to start."

He was right. I got off the phone, called the airlines, and made a reservation. Then I called my dad and told him I needed him to pick me up from the airport in New Orleans at 11:30 that night. I called Jerome back to let him know what I'd done, and then I contacted the owner of the salon to get personal time off for the rest of the week. I told him I needed to go to Louisiana to help my dad go through my grandmother's belongings after her death. I called her "Grams." She spent the summers with us when I was living with my dad.

That Grams had just died was true. The rest of it, not so much.

I went home, threw some clothes in a bag, and got something to eat with Bethany before she took me to Love Field Airport.

It happened just that fast.

On the drive from the airport to Slidell, I told dad about my plan to take what I'd been doing where I worked and, with Jerome, find a salon owner in Louisiana who might be willing to partner with us to take our successful model, make some changes, and make a whole lot more money, or just sell to us outright. Along the way, I'm sure I insinuated that I could use some seed money to get started. But I never got the chance to ask him outright for help.

"If me giving you money is part of your plan," he told me, "then you need a different plan."

I guess I shouldn't have been surprised at that, either. After all, I'd turned down his earlier offer for financial help to further my education, so why would he give me any money now to use to start a new business?

The next day, I met with Susie, a girl I remembered from high school, a pretty, cheerleader-type who never gave me the time of day back then when I was a dopehead. She had been working at a tanning salon in Slidell for several years. I told her what I'd been doing, where I worked in Dallas, the size of our company, and that I was hoping to find somebody that I could partner with that would be open to making a whole lot more money but would be required to make a lot of changes.

However, my franchise-based system was completely different from the one used at her salon. Mine was predicated on volume, membership, and constant money flow. Hers was seasonal. They charged more during busy times and then rode it out in the slower months.

She said my model would never work in Slidell, but she told me about a place in Baton Rouge called Tiger Tan that had been open for about a year and apparently wasn't doing well. "Maybe you could give them a call," she suggested.

Our visit ended, and I headed from there to the library and jotted down the phone numbers from every tanning salon in the state. Back at my dad's, I started making calls. I was well familiar with the standard sales process: make 100 calls to get 10 appointments and make one sale—if you're fortunate.

I made calls for two solid days. Nothing.

Then I remembered Susie's recommendation: Tiger Tan. It hadn't been among the numbers listed in the phone books at the library.

I called, got the owner's fiancé on the phone, and told her my plan.

"Let me call you right back," she said.

Moments later, I presume after talking to her husband-to-be, we set up a meeting for the very next day.

As the name suggested, Tiger Tan was located near the campus of Louisiana State University (LSU). Their main clientele were college students. Bryant and his fiancé, Linda, were concerned about financing. But within a couple of weeks, after I returned home, I had convinced Bryant to come visit me in Dallas and see how my company there operated. He did, and he liked what he saw.

In late October, we made a deal. "This is what I'm going to do," he said. "You give me $1,575 as a down payment, and at the end of the first month, if you give me a $10,000 check, it is yours." We agreed to a purchase price of $75,000 payable over 24 months, but the store wasn't worth a fraction of that before we took over.

Jerome put in his half of the down payment, Bethany and I moved to Baton Rouge in December—and at the end of that first month, January 1993, Jerome and I made almost $30,000 in memberships. Bryant got his $10,000, and Tiger Tan made even more money in the spring. Within six months, we bought out a competitor on the other end of the LSU campus.

Later, after I had bought and completely paid for Tiger Tan, Bryant said, "What you have done has really been impressive."

I smiled. "Man, I didn't have anything to lose."

"No, you're wrong," he replied. "You had everything to lose."

I realized he was correct. I was on parole. I had to transfer my parole and move my life. I did it on sheer faith in my ability to make what I thought was working in Dallas work in Baton Rouge.

I'd always thought Bryant was the one that had everything to lose. Just the opposite was true.

Everything did not end well for me and Jerome. In fact, we went our separate ways at the end of that first year because of a disagreement. I kept Tiger Tan and the debt it held at that time. He took the other location debt free.

But I felt great. I liked what I was doing. My self-confidence was growing.

Doug Pollock was on the upswing.

Shame it didn't stay that way.

CHAPTER FOUR

—

Bottoming Out

TIGER TAN BROUGHT WITH IT a lifestyle I'd never experienced before and couldn't get enough of. It sucked me in and ultimately spit me out.

LSU was a 24/7 party, and since a good portion of our clients were college girls, I'd go on and around campus promoting our business—and partying. By the summer of 1993, Mark had moved to Baton Rouge to work at the salon, as did Jerome's former assistant manager, Bill. I had actually largely stayed away from doing or selling any drugs for a while, but when Bill arrived from Dallas with some pot, that drew me back in.

From that day onward, I started using again.

At the same time, Bethany was starting to become unhappy with me, and who could blame her? When I wasn't working, I was going out every night of the week drinking and getting high. There were bars everywhere. Meanwhile, here she was in Louisiana, far away from her home back in Pittsburgh, and she didn't have any friends. Still, when she told me in November that she didn't want to live together any longer, it somehow caught me off guard.

When she left to stay with a colleague from work for a couple of weeks, I pulled every trick in the book to get her to come back: dinner, flowers, you name it. It worked, too, but when she returned, it was more like a friendship to me than anything else. As I continued to wine and dine Bethany, it provided the attention she'd wanted all along, and she recommitted herself to a relationship with me. Yet when she did that, I went the opposite direction.

I wasn't ready to settle down. It scared me. I figured if I ever did, I'd probably screw it up. It was easier to be done with it than to drag it out. So, I turned up my bad boy stuff to the highest level. I went out every night, stayed out, and didn't come home. I slept around with other girls like crazy. I basically went wild.

It went on like that for about a month-and-a-half until I went out one Sunday to go drinking with some friends on a boat. When I got home, I walked into the bedroom, bent over to take off my shoes, and noticed the closet door open and her side completely empty.

Bethany had left. I just sat there, dumbfounded by something I should've known was coming.

That was February 1994. Bethany and I had been trying to figure out how to make it work, but in the midst of it all, I found something that I liked a whole lot more than being in the relationship: the college party life and the girls that came with it. I had crossed the line, and I didn't want to come back over.

I spoke with Bethany a little after that, but I was through. She was through. Eventually, she moved back to Pittsburgh.

From then on, the downward progression continued. I went from smoking pot to once again eating a lot of Ecstasy. I also started going back to Dallas more often to visit friends and other partiers I never knew before, and I started hanging out with them. On those trips, I'd visit mom, whose health was only getting worse, and I'd almost always try to go see my daughter, too. It was never as dad, though. It was always just as Doug.

It was easy for me to keep the party going. Tiger Tan was growing, we remodeled the salon, and I had developed a little workforce that included Mark and a girl who was a student that was sweet on him. Mark and I lived together after Bethany left. While I was manager of the salon, it pretty much ran itself, and I got to the point where I neglected a lot of my responsibilities. I could leave on a Thursday and come back on Monday. During the slower time of the years, such as from mid-May through mid-August when school was out, I had to try and work a little bit harder, but sometimes I didn't even do it then.

I just couldn't stop. People called me the Energizer Bunny. I kept going and going.

Upswing Doug was long gone. Dopehead Doug was back and coming on strong, just in time for my personal life to become even more chaotic.

~~~~

When I met Shannon, she was a customer at Tiger Tan. We started dating after her marriage to a guy in Virginia went south. I was not only attracted to Shannon, I thought she was angelic. She was so good, defined by my perception of her character and maturity, that it frightened me. She drank some, but she didn't do drugs, and she generally wasn't a party girl. In fact, Shannon went to church, and even got me going to church with her.

However, I was again the bad boy to her good girl, and I quickly discovered her halo had a decidedly sensual flaw. Essentially, she believed everything the Bible said was true—except for the part about not having sex before marriage.

I was only too happy to oblige.

Before long, she became my girlfriend, and when we made visits to Dallas together, I spent most of my time with her instead of with my mom or my daughter. Over the next year, we got really serious, and I would've sworn I was going to marry her—except that I met another girl, Melissa, on Memorial Day weekend 1995 when Shannon and I went to the Lake of the Ozarks in Missouri for a big party. Unlike Shannon, Melissa liked to party and have a good time. Little did I know then how quickly Melissa could go from good to bad to worse.

It was there that I also first tried GHB, better known as the "date rape" drug, but I never used it for that purpose. It was its ability to give me a deep, restful sleep so I could go all night if I wanted to that eventually made it my drug of choice. After that weekend, I began hanging out and partying with a group that included Melissa whenever I went to Dallas and Shannon wasn't with me.

I played both sides, and I kept it up until later that summer. Somehow, maybe through women's intuition, Shannon found out about Melissa and the rest of the group, and she wasn't happy about it. Then again, Shannon and I had started growing apart by then, and I suspected she was seeing someone on the side in Houston. Not long after that, Shannon told me we needed some time apart; specifically, six months.

"In six *weeks*, I might not remember your name," I wisecracked, "So six months is way too long. We might want to try 30 days."

Shannon angrily agreed—and as that was playing itself out, on my next trip to Dallas, I went to see my mother.

~~~~

It was the Sunday before Labor Day, and we had the best visit. It was the most alive and vibrant I'd seen mom in a long time. We talked about all kinds of stuff. We cut up and laughed and joked. It was a really fun. The next morning, I stopped in to see her again on my way out to return to Baton Rouge.

It was nothing like the day before. She was weak and listless. It frightened me.

Quietly, she told me, "I'm going to see my daddy."

"Yeah, I know," I replied, not entirely sure what mom meant.

Then she added, "I'm going to see my other daddy, too."

No, I thought. *She means God. Her Abba Father.*

I knew when I left that day that it would be the last time I ever saw her alive.

I responded to the sense of impending loss by escaping into several days and nights of partying in celebration of Mark's birthday. Then, Friday at 2:30 a.m., Mark and I came home from the club, only to hear a message on the answering machine from our sister, Penny.

"If you want to see mom alive again, you need to get to Dallas today."

Right away, he and I scored some dope, found somebody to open and close Tiger Tan, and left. A buddy volunteered to come with us and drive.

We got to Dallas, showered at a friend's apartment, and went straight to the hospital. Penny, My Ma, my Aunt Debbie, and a few other extended family members and friends were there.

I had been up for a few days without sleeping. I was high and out of my mind. I couldn't even compel myself to go into mom's room. I didn't want to see her like that after our last conversation the weekend before. I just couldn't.

A doctor came over to us. "Your mom is on life support. Somebody needs to make the decision."

Everyone looked at me, Penny, and Mark—her three kids—and my siblings looked at me, the moment too overwhelming for them.

"Do you want *me* to make the decision?" I asked.

"Well, I'm not making it," Penny said, devastated.

The three of us stepped away from everyone else and huddled—and we just knew. She had suffered for so long.

I took a deep breath and turned to the doctor. It's not often that you have the balance of someone's life in your hands, much less your mother's. It's a terrible thing.

"We need to take her off life support," I said.

She passed away minutes later.

My mother died September 9, 1995.

Mom's funeral was scheduled, and I called my dad and asked if he was coming. "I really need you to be here," I pleaded. I'd rarely before felt that I needed my father's emotional support, but this was one moment when I did.

He said he couldn't do it.

I should've understood, but I couldn't. Not then.

I was so hurt, that was the last time I talked to him for the next six months.

I then called Shannon and asked her to come. She refused, too.

In the end, it was Melissa who ended up providing my brother and I a place to stay and helping us both over the next several days and through mom's funeral.

Eventually, Mark and I returned to Baton Rouge. When Shannon and I saw one another next, it was at the end of our 30-day break, and by then, Shannon had apparently gotten in touch with Melissa and confronted her about me. Everything was quickly unraveling.

Shannon and I went to my place. I thought it was just to talk, but she had something else in mind. After we were finished, she got out of the bed and put on her clothes.

"What are you doing?" I asked.

"I thought that by spending 30 days apart, you'd make some progress. All you've done is regress. I'm gone."

I was incredulous. *After all I've just been through,* I thought. *You just used me.*

I was still fresh off the loss of my mom, and I'd spent a good part of those 30 days in Dallas with Melissa, which hadn't set well with Shannon. While I did not sleep with

Melissa during that time, I was wild with other girls, partially for the fun of it, but mostly to numb my pain.

Yet none of them mattered to me because my heart was starting to turn toward Melissa.

I even thought I was falling in love with her—at least kind of, anyway.

I was such a mess.

It was going to get worse, too.

~~~~

The rest of 1995 and into 1996, my life unraveled further. I was arrested twice. One incident came when Melissa was flying into New Orleans from Dallas so that we could take a trip together for spring break to Florida. On the way to the airport, I passed out at a stoplight with my car in drive after taking too much GHB. I came to when I heard the sirens and saw everybody but the National Guard pulling up: cops, paramedics, firemen, you name it.

I quickly hid the GHB, but I had a backpack in the back of the car with a tin full of the finest pot that I had planned to take on our trip. I ended up having to go to the hospital, while Mark went to pick up Melissa for me.

I was charged with possession of marijuana. When I later went to court, I came away with a misdemeanor probation instead of a felony. Thanks to Tiger Tan, I had good money, I bought a good attorney, and, I guess, got some good luck with it.

The second arrest occurred when two undercover police officers showed up outside my apartment, brought there by a complaint from a neighbor and drawn over by the smell of pot wafting out my open front door. They knocked, but the odor was all the reasonable cause they needed to come inside.

They searched the place and found marijuana, Valium, and Xanax. I was charged with felony possession of all three drugs, but I wasn't in jail long. Within 24 hours, I posted bond and was released.

Most people who do drugs can't afford the drugs. That was never my problem. I could afford to do and sell the drugs (and pay for the attorney and the bond, too)—and that *was* a problem.

I remember making all kinds of promises to myself while I was sitting in that cell. I was starting to realize the path I was on was going to send me back to prison, maybe for good. I even prayed and cut a deal with the Lord. "God, I won't do this again. I promise." But I got myself out fast—and freedom made me quickly forget about any prayers or promises.

Meanwhile, Melissa and I had begun a long-distance relationship that progressed to her moving to Baton Rouge to be with me and to go to school. She was studying to become a court reporter, ironically enough, and she took classes at an area community college. When she moved, my brother got his own place, and Melissa and I got a townhome close to LSU.

Her decision to come live with me was also predicated on me making a commitment to her, so one day as we were driving together, she declared, "I'm not moving here unless you are going to marry me." I don't know what motivated her to say that. We were both so stupid, and we never talked about anything long term or what that really meant. We just got together and had a good time. We thought that was all there was to it.

Nevertheless, I immediately made a U-turn, and we went straight to the jewelry story. She picked out a ring that she wanted, and that was that.

The commitment issues I'd had with Bethany and Shannon were tossed aside.

I was going to marry Melissa.

We got a townhome together and began what would turn out to be a year-and-a-half-long engagement as 1996 rolled into 1997—but it was anything but blissful. I was so wild. She was so wild. We both pushed each other's buttons in a bad way. I also found out Melissa had the nastiest temper when she drank. I used to say I thought it was because she was drinking and taking Prozac, but I can't tell you if that's 100 percent accurate. Maybe it was just me that made her crazy and mean. It was always horrible.

One time, for example, on a weekend getaway to San Antonio, we were staying at a hotel near the River Walk downtown. We went out, had some drinks, did some dancing, and came back to the hotel. I left the room to go down to the vending machines and get something, and when I returned, I guess she had passed out. I knocked and knocked on the door until I went to the lobby and called up to the room.

When she finally opened the door, I went in, and she went off! Before I could turn around, a beer bottle went buzzing by my head. I ducked, put my arm up, and it careened off my hand and against the little hallway wall.

That was typical of our exchanges. She was always physical, and whenever she'd start yelling, I always slapped my hand over her mouth. "Be quiet! The cops are going to come!" Then she'd get away and *call* the cops or my parole officer. She was vindictive. There were probably a dozen different times that she'd take off the engagement ring—the one I U-turned to buy for her—and throw it across the parking lot. I'd be out there, time and again, in the middle of the night trying to find that ring.

It was ridiculous—and all of this was *before* we got married.

Why in the world we stayed together is a great question with no good answer. There's no doubt Melissa and I were negatively co-dependent. I was doing and selling drugs. She was depressed and drinking. We constantly made each other feel jealous. When she wanted to fight, I often disengaged, leaving for days. That infuriated her, and what she did infuriated me. It was like each one of us was holding a torch, and we threw gas on one another.

I know, too, that when I committed to marry Melissa, I was not only trying to overcome my previous poor track record with women. I was also making that commitment based on how badly my mom and dad's divorce had hurt me. In fact, I had made two verbal vows growing up. One was to never, ever put a needle in my arm and shoot up because I saw my parents do it.

The other was to never get a divorce.

I had spent my whole life telling myself that, and now that I was engaged, I was determined to see it through—no matter what.

It is important to be aware of the inner vows and other messages we allow to play in our minds and hearts. Many are quite beneficial. But you never know when one might come back to bite you.

~~~~

Melissa and I got married on December 7, 1997—and I still call it *my* day that will live in infamy, considering it had all the fireworks of Japan's surprise attack on Pearl Harbor in 1941. The prelude to the attack came the night before when Mark and his girlfriend got into an argument at the hotel after the rehearsal dinner. They fought, and the cops were called, but he was allowed to stay the night. That only set the stage for the following night when, after the wedding ceremony, he and his girlfriend got so bad they were kicked out because they were disturbing the other guests at the hotel.

Apparently, that included Melissa. After we exchanged our vows and she had plenty of quality time at the open bar at the reception, we went up to our room. I had been drinking all day, which wasn't anything new, but I wasn't stupid and mean. I just drank to have fun. I never got the sloppy or slurring kind of drunk that Melissa did. Still, there we were, both intoxicated, when a hotel worker knocked on our door.

He informed us that Mark was being told to leave, and I told Melissa I needed to go check on him.

Boom! Before I could even think of leaving, Melissa launched her attack, running her mouth about my brother.

I don't even remember what she said, but I didn't like it. We argued, and she again got violent with me. This time, though, just like the first wave of Japanese Zeros at Pearl Harbor, Melissa suddenly decided to leave, presumably to go back down to the bar and regroup before returning to dive bomb me once more.

I wasn't going to give her the chance. I'd taken enough damage for one night.

I took Melissa's bags, threw them out in the hall, and locked her out.

I wasn't done. After going down and trying to find her to no avail, I went to Melissa's bridesmaid and spent the rest of the evening with her. We got a little touchy feely with each other, but that was it. We didn't have sex. Nevertheless, I didn't get back to our room until 5:00 the next morning.

Melissa was not there. I was surprised, but it was also okay. It saved me from having to tell her where I'd been.

I went to sleep—but I was convinced. When I woke up, I was going to head straight to Dallas by myself, go on the skiing trip to Beaver Creek, Colorado that Melissa and I had planned for our honeymoon by myself, and then, when I got back, I was going to get an annulment so that it would be as though the marriage never existed. I assumed an annulment to simply cancel the marriage was an option, as opposed to a divorce, because we had not "consummated" the marriage. I didn't realize that, in Louisiana, an annulment for that reason was not possible under any circumstances.

Whatever. I'd be better off without Melissa.

War over.

Of course, that's not how it turned out. The next morning, my dad and stepmother came to our room and talked to us. I told them my intentions in no uncertain terms. Melissa just stayed quiet. When I think about it now, she might have been guilty about something. Who knows? I think she might have been putting a few fake tears out there.

"No, Doug, you can't do that," they said regarding my plans.

"Watch me," I countered.

I was adamant, but not adamant enough. When it was all over, they'd convinced both of us that we'd come this far, so we might as well see it out. No better reason to begin life together as husband and wife, right?

We packed up our things and drove like crazy to get to Dallas on time for the flight to Colorado.

We were off on our honeymoon, happy couple that we were—and, incredibly, we had a great four days together in the Rocky Mountains. That was probably because we chose not to go to any clubs while we there. Instead, we spent a lot of time on the slopes, and we stayed in our resort room when we weren't skiing. I'd never skied before, and I enjoyed it to no end. It snowed for most of the trip. It was peaceful and unlike anything I'd ever experienced before in the deep south.

Our wedding night tirade was all but forgotten.

A few weeks after we returned home, we moved from our townhome to a house located in the same neighborhood where former Tiger Tan owners Bryant and Linda lived. The move itself took an ugly turn when, after everything had been packed up and taken away, I took one last little trek upstairs—and discovered a brown paper bag. Wondering where it had come from and how we had missed it, earlier, I started looking through it.

As I pulled out its contents, which included a couple of costumes with their particular accessories, I had a startling revelation.

Holy crap! I married a stripper!

I stormed downstairs and found Melissa.

"What is this?" I waved one of the risqué outfits in front of me. "I know you didn't wear this when you were a cocktail waitress. These are stripper clothes!"

She got that deer in the headlights look that said, "He knows."

I didn't let up. "We are not about to move out of this townhome and start a life in this house without me knowing the truth!"

I wanted to divorce her right then. That was how revolting what she'd done was to me.

Melissa insisted that she worked at a place called New Orleans Nights to help pay for her school. It was a strip bar in Fort Worth and a pretty high-class place, or so she insisted. "I was a cocktail waitress," she added. "I was only there a few months to make extra money."

I didn't believe her. *She'd probably been there the entire time before she moved to Baton Rouge.*

Infuriated, I took the bag into the back yard and lit it on fire.

I might bring all kinds of drugs into our house, but I sure as hell wasn't going to allow that inside our house.

I had such an issue with strippers. Maybe it was because Penny did it for a while, and I didn't like it. More than that, the majority of the girls or women who I encountered that were strippers had an air about themselves that they were man hustlers. They'd trick someone out of all their money with their lap dances and drinks and fake boobs and blonde hair.

That made me so mad.

Melissa and I got past it, just as we had all the arguments before, and the first couple of months or so at the new house were pretty much chaos free. One reason was because I was trying to cold knuckle and not sleep around. I had only been with Melissa since we got married, and that actually had a positive effect on me. Whenever I heard people talk about another person's integrity and character, I'd silently think, *I hope that's me someday.* I had aspirations to do more, to be better, and to make changes. Turning those aspirations into reality was a whole other thing.

Another reason was that we didn't have a fight. We had a couple of disagreements, of course, but for whatever reason, they didn't escalate. We were both really trying to play house the right way. I know, too, that I was keeping myself busy. I had yard projects to do and a pool to put in, so that kept me off the streets and away from things that usually upset Melissa. We also did stuff with Bryant and Linda, hanging out like normal married couples do.

All of that probably helped. But the lull was short lived.

As soon as we had our first big fight, everything reverted to the way it was before—and I mean everything. She drank, got angry, and lost it on me. I'd leave, go get high on pot, Ecstasy, or Xanax, and then go have sex with someone. I had a few "friends with benefits" for that purpose. Doing my own thing was my escape, the way I forgot about my problems with Melissa. I usually stayed out all night and came home before the sun came up.

Throughout the spring, summer, and into the fall of 1998, that's how life was. It was insane, and it heightened my desire to numb it all away with sex and drugs.

That's probably why I chose to use cocaine again.

~~~~~

It happened during a camping trip in late 1998. Hunting season was on, and some friends and I went to a 1,500-acre hunting camp on a friend's family property in Liberty, Mississippi to camp overnight before hunting the next day and evening. I was on parole, and I could not legally own a gun, so I was there to hang out and maybe fire off a round or two on someone's rifle just for fun.

We were in a little cabin with an open living room, sitting at a table by the stone fireplace, drunk and playing poker. I'd been coming up big all night, winning several hands. I was relaxed and having a good time.

That's when one of the fellas said, "Let's go get some blow!" One of them knew a guy nicknamed Main (probably short for "the main man") who agreed to meet us at a gas station on the outskirts of Baton Rouge and set us up.

"I'll drive," I said, knowing it was going to take a while to get there and back.

That was all I planned to do. I'd never done cocaine with any of these guys. They knew that was what had sent me to prison in the first place. But then, when we got there and everybody was putting their money in, I thought, *Why not me?*

"I'm in!"

Everybody was surprised, but we made the transaction and returned to the campsite with the goods.

I still kept my promise to myself. I didn't shoot up. But I snorted it.

It was good coke. No, it was great.

Main became my regular cocaine dealer after that night. He'd keep supplying me for the next year-and-a-half.

From then on, Melissa and I went from bad to worse to whatever is beyond worse. She stated calling my parole officer on me when she drank. She called the cops on me when she drank. She did all kinds of crazy stuff—when she drank.

On my end, I'd stopped smoking pot because I knew I'd have to pee in a cup every few weeks. It was a requirement of the random tests that were made part of my probation, and I knew I'd been smoking so much pot that it would stay in my system for 30 days or more. Cocaine, on the other hand, would typically be detectible for two or three days, though drinking could slow its elimination from the body. Sometimes it would seem like I'd never have clean urine. I figured I could duck and dodge for four or five days before I'd have to take a test. I still used everything else, especially the GHB, which at that time wouldn't show up in a drug test.

I was also dealing drugs, too, just small-time stuff. I'd buy something for this price and sell it for that price and make a few dollars here or there. I still had a little hustle in me. But after the cocaine use returned, people found out I knew where to get it, and in combination with the Ecstasy and the other drugs I could get, dealing turned into a full-fledged business.

That was ironic, considering that by early 2000, I was in the process of consolidating the two Tiger Tan locations that I had (I got the second location right after Melissa and I got married) and securing the funds and the site to open one big mega salon. Things only started getting crazier as I oversaw the transition at my legitimate business while trying to run my illegitimate enterprise.

The final thing that pushed me over the edge was when I found out Melissa was cheating on me. The fact that she was finally doing to me what I had been doing to her for a long time didn't matter. I still hated what she did. I moved out of the house for six months, giving up everything I owned in the process and letting her have the house. She didn't want to separate. She wanted to stay together and be miserable. I really didn't want that, and I knew that to make the separation happen, I was going to have to be the one to leave. That meant that I had to continue paying for the mortgage because it was in my name. Melissa then went and took all the money out of the bank account.

She beat me to the punch on a few things. I really underestimated her. She made life tough for me, that's for sure—and I am certain I did the same for her.

I moved in with two guys that were in college and lived on the LSU campus. They were younger than I was, they drank and partied—and I turned their world upside down. It went from zero to 1,000. Cocktails, coke, weed, Ecstasy, GHB. It went nonstop, 24/7, for six months.

I just quit caring.

I didn't care about anything.

~~~~~

Divorce proceedings got underway. I had spent my whole life telling myself I would never get a divorce. But with Melissa, we could never break the destructive cycle, and I got to a place where I knew that if I was going to spend the money to initiate a divorce process, I wouldn't stop until I finished.

I thought back to my Aunt Debbie, who I'd idolized as an amazing Christian woman. About that same time, her and her husband got a divorce. Here was a woman who helped raise me. She didn't leave him. He left her. But after that, I said to myself, "Okay. If my aunt can get a divorce, as godly as she is, then as ungodly as I am, I need to get one, too."

I took on a new girlfriend, too—Jenny, a Tiger Tan client who was also on the LSU Golden Girl dance line that performed with the band. She was young, pretty, and dove right in to the drugs and the partying with me. She wasn't really on my radar, but after I separated from Melissa, we started hanging out and talking. Before long, I began flirting, and that was that.

Then there was the cocaine. It is so addictive. It led me to places I never thought I would go, and I did things I never thought I would have done. I stayed up all night for days on end. It got to the point that I was basically driving myself crazy. I had tapped the phones at our house. I hired a private investigator. I thought one of my neighbors was trying to sleep with Melissa, too.

It was sick stuff.

January 2001 arrived, and in a desperate attempt to pull my life out of a tailspin, I had made some New Year's resolutions that I wasn't going to deal any more drugs. Instead, I was going to start refocusing on my business. I had taken the two locations near LSU, closed them down, and started the process of transferring all the equipment to the new, larger space located at the opposite end of the shopping strip from the original Tiger Tan.

My goal was to get the new place opened in time for the spring tanning season. It wasn't easy. Mark had been in jail for a couple of months after another drunk driving violation, so I had lost my right-hand man. I realized I was going to have to shape up or ship out. I was not in good shape to do that, but I had to convince myself I was. I had to salvage my reputation from the crappy one it had become over the past couple of years.

Meanwhile, I went to court for the final divorce settlement. It had gotten so ugly, and I had been committed to never let Melissa get anything from me monetarily. My attorney told me her demands. I don't think it was much, maybe $20,000, but I was so done.

I told my lawyer I'd pay it, and I asked for ten days to come up with the money.

My attorney looked at me. "Doug, I'm telling you right now, I don't want to know what you are going to do, but I have a good idea—and you don't need to do that. We can keep fighting this."

"No," I insisted. "Just give me ten days."

I made some phone calls. That weekend, I was going to get it done.

But that was going to be it.

The last deal.

After that, I was going to move on.

That Thursday night, I went out partying and having fun. I did some cocaine and GHB, and I popped a whole bunch of Ecstasy. I was on this up and down ride of get high, get up, get down, and do it all over again. I was flying high again on my own buzz.

Then, at about 8:00 p.m., I got a call from one of my regular connections who I had previously bought from and sold to, saying there were some college guys in from Natchitoches, Louisiana who wanted to buy every drug I had. Right away.

That wasn't really so uncommon—but it also seemed a bit too good to be true, especially when I considered the short notice. "But I'm not going to do anything until tomorrow," I told them.

He was insistent. "They're only here for the evening. I'll get everything from you on their behalf and take care of getting it to them."

I thought about it. In my drug-induced haze, it sure sounded good.

I took the bait.

"Okay. I'll meet you at midnight." We agreed to meet at the original Tiger Tan salon, which was still being unloaded for the move to the new location.

My connection, Eric, was there, along with a couple of others he and I knew. We went inside and snorted some coke. I kept the lights off, which allowed me to see outside without anyone being able to see in through the tinted windows. I noticed that there seemed to be more activity than usual in the parking lot and on the nearby streets.

That, along with Eric's nervous fidgetiness, should've been a warning sign to me, but by then I was going off the rails I was so crazy on the chemicals coursing through my body.

After a few more minutes, I got to business.

"So, how much dope do you want to buy?"

Eric said, "Just a couple of eight balls."

Based on the call a few hours back, I was expecting the mother lode. "A couple of eight balls? Man, what happened to all the stuff you wanted me to have for those other guys?"

He shrugged. "They ended up going back to Natchitoches because it was taking too long. But we want to get a couple of eight balls."

You'd think with all the cocaine in my system I would've instantly been paranoid, but I wasn't. I don't know. I guess I was just being trusting—which you can't do in the drug game.

I took another look outside, and the traffic and other activity had subsided. If this was a setup, I thought it was the perfect time to flip the script and walk out while I could.

"Here it is," I said, getting out the eight balls. "Leave the money on the counter. Lock the door on your way out."

As I hopped into my truck, I felt like I could bark at the moon I was so over the mountain high—but my senses were starting to kick in, too, if only just a bit.

Assuming Eric or one of the others were wired with sound, I thought, *we were talking, making a drug transaction, and then I was gone. It may have been just a shot in the dark, but I'll bet nobody was prepared for that, not even the cops.*

I pulled out and headed down the road. I turned on the radio, some Ozzy song was blaring, and I got lost in my own little trance.

Then, out of the corner of my right peripheral vision, I saw a red and blue streak.

I thought I was tripping.

The next second, I saw squad cars starting to block the intersection ahead, their lights flashing, while other cars began pinning me into a turn lane with a high curb.

It wasn't the drugs.

This is for real! It's a raid!

I had the dope and money in a bank bag, and I stuffed everything in the seat pocket hoping they wouldn't find it.

They pulled guns and drew down on me.

I got out and surrendered.

To the very end, including that fateful meeting with Eric and the others, I was a believer that there was still good even in the worst of people, that no one would set me up—not again. But looking back now, I was the one breaking all the rules. I knew the writing was on the wall for me. It was coming. If it hadn't come that night, it might well have come the next.

Running out of time, it was just a matter of when.

~~~~~

I was held in a parish jail for six months before my court date—but that was the bust that led to my appearance before the black-robed judge.

To the 30-year sentence that was reduced to 20, with the first 10 years spent behind bars.

To my audacious declaration of how that time was going to serve me—and my realization that day that I could have a 20-year prison sentence and still be successful.

Yet there was no way I could've foreseen how things ultimately played themselves out.

CHAPTER FIVE

NOWHERE TO GO
BUT UP

IMMEDIATELY AFTER MY CONVICTION, I was convinced life was really going to change for the better. But that optimism quickly waned as I was held in a correctional center for another seven months before ending up where I'd stay, at Forcht-Wade Correctional Center, in February 2003. I was in a little eight-by-eight-foot cell block with two bunks, a toilet, and a sink until I was later moved to a large dormitory with 40-50 men all together in the same space.

During that time of being bounced around, and into the spring of 2003, I'd managed, even from behind bars, to keep the new Tiger Tan open for business, thanks to help (at least, that's what I thought it was) from Jenny and Mark.

Then somebody sent me a write up from the LSU campus newspaper. The article described how I had been busted and that Tiger Tan was shutting down.

There's no telling how it happened. I assume a client told the newspaper that it was closing, the reporter looked into it, and the reporter did what reporters do. It was so embarrassing. Even worse, Jenny, who I had not heard from for quite a while, had taped up all the windows with newspaper so nobody could see in while she packed everything up and moved everything out.

Jenny shut it down and took me for all I had, which wasn't very much—but I saw my business as being my last hope in the free world. It was where I had placed my identity and sense of self-worth. There, and in the crazy lifestyle I'd been living.

Now it was all gone.

At that point, all contact with everybody I thought would have been there for me, friends that I ran around with or partied with, was non-existent. I'd figured they would stay in touch after all I'd done for them, but they forgot all about me. Oddly, it was clients from Tiger Tan—Lisa, Darla, and Michael and his daughter—who wrote me letters and tried to encourage me. They were the unlikely people, outside of my family, who stood by me.

As for family, I called dad once a week, and occasionally talked to my stepmom, Aimee, or Penny. We only got a 15-minute call, so the visits were brief. Penny wrote letters, too, and sent pictures of stuff she did in California training horses or of her family on vacation. I don't know why people behind bars want pictures of everything we want to see or do but can't while we're in prison, but I sure wanted them. They allowed me to live vicariously through the lives of others, at least for a few moments at a time.

Photos of me, either with my daughter or with my mom, were by far the most meaningful. I had one of me sitting behind a drum set with my mom standing over me smiling ear to ear. Another had her next to me while I was standing at a full-fledged xylophone. In that one, I had on an Acapulco t-shirt with a sailfish on it. I was probably eight or nine in those pictures. I also had a photo of me with my daughter when she was four or five that was taken on one of my sporadic visits to Dallas. We were standing in front of the purple Toyota Celica that I had at the time. That particular photo had likely been sent to me at some point by Jenny.

Mark was in touch sometimes, too. He was in San Antonio, trying to get himself together and his addiction to alcohol under control. We'd actually spent time in jail together for about two months while I was waiting to be sentenced. It was sad, but that was when we got to know each other in a different way. It was probably the first time in our adult lives that we were both sober at the same time. We still had a little junk left inside that needed to work itself out. That's when he told me he had stolen a lot of money from me, and I told him how I took advantage of him in the way I had him work for me at Tiger Tan. We both came clean about some stuff.

Some people might try to ascribe it to jailhouse religion, but our time also centered around studying the Bible together, something else we had never done together before. We read it and talked about it. I had an NIV Life Application Study Bible, but I didn't know enough about it to gravitate to the Old Testament, the New Testament, or the Psalms. We just bounced all over the place. When he was released, Mark first went to a halfway house in Dallas for about six months before I convinced him to return to Baton Rouge to again help run Tiger Tan with Jenny, which they did until it all fell apart.

I'd lost it all. My house was probably the first thing to go; the business was the last thing to go. Jenny took whatever clothing, jewelry, or other personal possessions I had. I was completely broke, too. So, by June 2003, I had slipped into a deep state of depression. I had gone from telling the judge that I was going to prison to "not serve time but for time to serve me" to finding out Jenny had ripped me off (at least, that was what I told myself to make me feel better) and that my business was history.

But it was more than the girl. It was more than the loss of Tiger Tan.

It was like the final curtain call.

The world as I knew it was ending.

~~~~

At Forcht-Wade, my job was in the kitchen, where I cooked specific breakfast and lunch dishes for the prison administrators. Each morning, I woke up, read my Bible, and got on my knees and prayed. Next, I went to the bathroom, looked in the mirror, put water on my face, and prepared to go do my job. When I was done in the afternoon, I lifted weights and killed time until dinner. After the last meal, I was able to go outside and stay out until the lights were turned on or the yard was closed for the day.

I just found myself going through the motions, nothing more.

I walked the oval running track and listened to preaching and teaching messages on cassette by people like Kenneth Copeland, Jerry Saville, or Jesse Duplantis. I also listened to Christian music on cassette, be it Steven Curtis Chapman, Michael W. Smith, or Third Day. We had always played pop music at Tiger Tan, and techno club music was my favorite. But I wanted anything that was different and wasn't going to remind me of the life I had before. I didn't even watch TV unless it was a football game.

My mood wasn't changing, though. I had a devotional book by Kenneth and Gloria Copeland called *From Faith to Faith*. It talked about changing your routine to read more and pray more, and I tried that—but I just couldn't get my mind off of what had happened outside of prison. I was still trying to figure out how to hold onto this or save that when I actually had nothing out there to hold or save.

There was no joy in anything that I was doing, yet somehow I knew God was the answer. All the bits and pieces I had learned before about God were still there in my heart. I didn't know how to get to them yet, but I knew He was the key.

So, I prayed. I read my Bible. But I isolated myself. I didn't have any friends. I was doing it all solo, and it was a challenge.

One afternoon, I remember feeling so lonely and depressed, I finally said a simple prayer to the Lord. I was outside my dorm sitting on the ground with my back against the wall, looking out over a big field surrounded by razor wire. Right then, I got as transparent with God as I'd ever been before. I so desperately needed an answer.

"Lord," I said aloud, "I'm gonna have to serve all this time in prison, and I've got a long time to go, so I'm gonna need you to send me a friend. I am gonna need you to send me somebody that I can be accountable to you through, and they can be accountable to you through me, but mostly that we can be accountable to you together."

Then I added, as if for emphasis, "I have a long time to go, and it doesn't look like I'm going to be getting out. I can't do this on my own."

About two weeks later, this guy walked up to me in the prison yard by the basketball court.

"Is your name Doug Pollock?"

I'd never seen him before. *He must be new.* "That's me."

He smiled. "My name is John. Two weeks ago, I was at church, and a guard from the prison, who knew I was about to be sent here, came up to me and told me to be sure to find you. He told me you were really serving God, and we needed to get connected."

It seemed too good to believe, but here he was. Until that moment, I knew God had done some things for me, but a lot of that was in hindsight. This was not hindsight. This was perspective going forward.

"Man, it's about time you got here, because I told God two weeks ago that I needed a friend." We hugged. It was love at first sight. We even said that about ourselves to others, and you really don't say that about another guy in prison. But it was true!

John Skipworth requested to be placed in the same dorm I was, and we had bunks that were right beside each other. As we talked and got to know each other over the next several days, I learned that John was incarcerated for armed robbery. He had been in a 90-day program at Shreveport Community Church called Overcomers. The guard, Rivera, went to that church and was involved in the program. He had been talking to John, knew his story, and discovered he was about to be incarcerated at Forcht-Wade.

I knew Rivera, and I guess he had been watching me. I wouldn't have thought I stood out, but Rivera must have observed my daily routine, seen my consistency, and put it all together. Unlike the last time I was in prison in Texas, I had separated myself from the pack. I didn't get involved in fighting or any of the other foolishness. I was trying to do the right thing. Amazingly, despite my emotional struggles, it was obvious to Rivera that I was really trying to live out what I professed to believe.

How ironic it was for a guard to give a rat's rear end about anybody in prison. Yet Rivera recognized there was something different about me, and he knew John was going to be coming into this environment.

It was just beautiful. It really was a match made in heaven.

God answered my prayer.

I had my friend.

Still, even though I had just received a special delivery from God, I was still very depressed. I tried everything I could to shake it, but it was just so heavy. For many weeks, I struggled to even get out of my bunk. My mind remained consumed with everything I felt I had lost. I knew that if I didn't figure things out, my 10 years was going to seem like a life sentence.

A couple of weeks after John arrived, I woke up in the middle of the night. I realized John wasn't in his bed, so when I went to use the restroom, I looked over in the day-room area. He was there playing cards and smoking a cigarette. I didn't say anything. I went back to bed.

The next day he got up, and we had lunch. After that, I went up to him, "Man, let me tell you something. I prayed and asked the Lord to send me a friend, and I can tell you this. You are gonna have to decide if you are going to do the things you were doing last night—playing cards, smoking cigarettes, and hanging out with that group of folks—or not. You are not going to mess up my blessing, so you better get it straight."

He got it straight, and he kept it that way, so much so that one afternoon John came up and looked right at me. He said the Lord had showed him a vision. It was as if I was hanging on to a rope, sliding down from one knot to the other. He said he saw a clear image of my knuckles, as white as they could be, holding on to the knot with everything I had.

"You are trying to hold on to all this, and this is what is eating you up," John said. "You have to release it."

He didn't have to tell me what "it" was. I knew: the girlfriend, the old identity, and the stress that came along with trying to get something that I really didn't want but thought I did.

I had to let it all go.

I had to have faith and release my past to God.

<center>~~~~~</center>

That was when things started to change for me emotionally and spiritually. It wasn't immediate; in fact, I still couldn't get "undepressed," if that's a good term to use, to save my life. I'd pray, only to find myself needing to pray more. When it was hard to get up one day, I'd force myself to get up earlier the next day. Exercise is supposed to be good for depression, so I'd run around the prison yard in circles like a caged hamster on a wheel.

Morning after morning, I'd climb down out of that bunk, scuffle over to the sink, get the water going, splash some on my face, and look at myself. We didn't have mirrors, per se, just dull pieces of metal that really didn't give a good, clean reflection. But it was just enough of an image for me to see my face, its sad eyes staring back at me—and no smile.

I knew I had to do something to block out the voices—to, as John had said, release myself from their constant questioning, raising doubts that compounded on each other. "You're in prison. How are you ever gonna get back to that place where you were financially?" "How are you ever gonna get a new car?" "How are you ever gonna get a job that's gonna pay you what you need?"

One day, I took a long look at myself in that mirror. I didn't know who was nearby, and I really didn't care. The statement I made next, and the action I took to support it, by no means lined up with the reflection looking back at me—but it was definitely the day I began to become alive again.

I looked into my own eyes and spoke.

"Lord, I have no clue how I let myself get to this place, but if I'm ever going to get out of it, I'm going to have to put a smile on my face first. I don't feel like smiling—but I have to start trying."

I couldn't help but think that a lot of people talk to themselves in prison. *Maybe I am finally starting to fit in.* Next, I commanded my facial muscles to respond and put on that smile. It was fake as could be, and I knew that, but I did it anyway.

Then I walked away from that mirror, and throughout the rest of the day, I envisioned myself wearing that smile and told my muscles to do their thing.

For the next couple of months, that became my new daily routine, and I decided to stop feeding the depression monster with the negative self-talk that had sustained it despite everything else I had been doing: listening to Christian music and teaching, reading my Bible, and praying. At times, my anxiety was intense, realizing I was unable to control anything that had or was going on outside of those prison walls. I was in a rut—one that I sometimes didn't feel I'd ever climb out of. It nearly drove me crazy.

But I kept starving the monster—and I kept smiling.

Sometimes, especially when we don't feel like it, we have to do something different. For me, I had to unpack the lies I'd come to believe and replace them with truth, *believing* in something even when it wasn't what I saw staring back at me.

I can't tell you how long it took, perhaps a few months, but it was something someone said to me that let me know it was over. I was walking across the basketball court late one bright, cloudless morning when I saw Slim, a pleasant guy with wire-rimmed glasses and not quite all of his teeth, walking toward me. We were just crossing paths. I was going in one direction, and Slim was going in the other.

We passed, and then I heard Slim shout out, "Hey, Smiley!"

It caught me so off guard I stopped in my tracks. I looked around to see who he was talking to, but there was nobody out there but the two of us.

I looked at Slim. "Who, me?"

"Yes, you."

"Why did you call me Smiley?"

He responded, "You're always smiling!"

What you choose to believe is so important, even when it is not what you see. Without me actually realizing it until that moment, the fake smile had become a real one. The negative self-talk was silenced. The depression was gone. All the disciplines I'd been doing—listening to the right music, reading the Bible, praying, all of it—had finally paid off. The power to change was in my control, and it wasn't so much the disciplines, but the *belief* they birthed, that made the difference. I recalled that in 1 Corinthians 9:24-25 the Apostle Paul wrote, "Do you not know that in a race all the runners run, but only one gets the prize? Run in such a way as to get the prize. Everyone who competes in the games goes into strict training. They do it to get a crown that will not last, but we do it to get a crown that will last forever."

I felt like an athlete who had completed his training.

I had begun to believe what I wanted to become.

I'd finally let go of that rope John told me I'd been holding onto.

From then on, the transformation continued. Anytime I was given a job to do—endlessly sweeping the sidewalks, mopping the concrete, picking up cigarette butts, whatever it was—I did it with a new attitude. There was a 10-acre piece of overgrown land that I had to clear with a non-motorized thatching mower. It was brutal work, but I told myself, *These people are trying to break my spirit, but I'm just going to go out, exercise, and get in shape.* I just kept mowing. They had to make me stop. It was all a matter of the mind, and of turning that bad situation into a positive one.

Another thing that turned around had to do with my feelings of self-worth as a businessperson. I found out from Mark that Jenny had taken some of the tanning beds and put them in storage. I sold one of them for $400 to a girl whose brother was in the same prison dorm with me. What I did next with that money was a miracle. We had a hobby shop in prison where inmates could make leather goods, do woodcraft, and build furniture. I took that $400 and invested it in wood, paint, and materials. Then I began making clocks, jewelry boxes, and even heart-shaped plaques with roses on them that said, "I love you."

John joined me working with leather. For my birthday, he made me a leather Bible cover with a runner ending a race and breaking over the finish line, perfectly in line with the passage from 1 Corinthians 9. It replaced my original Bible cover that had a photo of an empty boat on a calm body of water with a violent thunderstorm in the background, illustrating peace in the storm. In prison, little things like inspiring Bible covers can be very motivational. John also made leather belts and purses.

I'm not a craftsman, but I asked others—usually old, cranky lifers who had already been locked up 25-30 years—to teach me how to make other items like rocking chairs. They were reluctant at first, but I was kind and polite, not typical of somebody in prison, and I wore them down until they eventually taught me what to do. If someone wrote down the steps for me, I was the kind of guy who could follow the instructions and get it done.

Five months later, I had started a business. Once I learned how to make something and wanted to produce a lot of them, I subbed the work out to other inmates. One of the first things I produced that way in mass quantities were the heart-shaped plaques. I cut out the patterns and glued, screwed, and craft coated them. I hired others to do the sanding and the airbrushing, though I later learned how to do the airbrushing myself. If there was something else I didn't like to build, but I knew it would sell, I paid somebody else to do it entirely.

When people came to visit the prison on weekends, I'd display and sell the items we made. I also began producing pieces for others I knew on the outside. I'd send one to them, mention how I was trying to sell them in prison, and they'd find others who wanted to buy one.

I continued my little enterprise throughout my time behind bars. We even had an annual arts and crafts show open to the public. The last year I was there, a TV reporter from Shreveport, Louisiana came out and interviewed me about what we were doing. As a result of that report, people started calling the prison to reserve items, especially my jewelry boxes and football-helmet shaped clocks. I actually made thousands of dollars. To this day, I have some of the most popular items I made in prison (including a helmet clock of the national champion LSU Tigers) hanging in my home.

～～～

The prison system is made up of a diverse, and often divisive, group of people. They're from this part of the state or that, from one neighborhood or the next. Inmates adhere to many belief systems, and some have no belief systems at all. There are groups of people who identify with one another and others who are completely at odds. Regardless of all that, everyone believes they are right. You can only imagine the conflicts that take place in such an environment. There is one thing we all have in common, though. Everyone wants to get released early. Stories spread like wildfire about how this person got their time cut, or how that person made parole. As inmates, we *lived* on the hope of getting out early, even when it was obvious that it was impossible.

Every day, various groups came to the prison to present or speak to us. Some were there to tell us about God and the things He'd done in their lives. Some of the stories were just so amazing they sounded too good to be true. But each one stirred something on the inside that I couldn't fully explain.

One night in early 2004, Lifeline Ministries from Monroe, Louisiana came in, and a feisty, confident guy named David Otis was the pastor. He brought his wife and began, "See this woman? That's my wife. Y'all go ahead and look at her. She is pretty, I know. Now that's enough. It's over with." That broke the ice with us.

Then Pastor Otis introduced the guest speaker, a man he'd brought in from Lifeline, who told us his story of how he had a 120-year prison sentence that should have kept him locked up until he died.

It was interesting. It was exciting. He was a good storyteller.

Then he shared how, through a chain of events, he was released from prison after only 15 years.

On all the other occasions when I heard similar stories, I told myself, "Man, I wish that would happen to me," or "I hope I can get a break like that."

But this night was different, and so was my self-talk. I clearly remember asking myself, "Why can't that happen to me?" I sat there for a few minutes, and then I said something else that would change my thinking in a radical way forever.

"Instead of, 'Why not me?' how about, 'Why not me!'"

The guest speaker had a miracle happen for him—and from that moment on, I believed not in a question, but a declaration that the impossible was created for me to make possible.

Of course, the prison system itself is also its own unique world. Unless they have or know someone behind bars, prison isn't something families talk about as they sit around the dinner table. They don't discuss prison politics, and they surely don't talk about the types of people who are in there. Over time, I've spoken to my family—wife, Kristin, and our kids, Michael and Hadley—about what it was like for me in prison, especially if something in the news prompts the conversation. Even with cases like that, prison life is simply not every day conversational fare for most people, and it's understandable.

Therefore, it's easy to stereotype those who have been in prison, and, even more so, those who are still in prison. When I was *in* prison, I found myself stereotyping people all the time. Just like practically everyone else, it was most often by how someone looked and most definitely by the crime they committed. After all, I wasn't locked up with a bunch of choir boys that got caught drinking their parent's liquor. There were murderers, drug dealers, and carjackers. There were some who committed home invasions and tied up everybody in the house just to get the code to an automated teller machine. There were others who had molested children. No, there were definitely no choir boys.

For a time, I'd hear what type of crimes others did and the sentences they had received for their crimes, and I'd find myself saying, if for no other reason than to complain about something, "I can't believe that they got less time than me."

I guess it was my way of trying to make myself feel better, but what it really did was keep me frustrated. On top of that, it made me look at people for what they did, which in turn would cause me to say and do things that I shouldn't.

One day between breakfast and lunch, I was talking to a fellow inmate, and he mentioned someone we knew who had just been placed into sex offender call out. That meant the person wouldn't acknowledge that they were going to these groups because they had committed a sex crime, but you knew they were meeting with these certain people at this certain time, so they had to have some sort of sex crime on their record.

He said, "You know that guy only got five years for molesting some kid?"

"That's bull crap!" I said, and I meant it. I was really upset. "I can't believe he did that and only got five years. They gave me 20 years!"

Right then, the Holy Spirit spoke to my heart. He reminded me of Psalm 37:1-4. In it, David wrote, "Don't worry about the wicked or envy those who do wrong. For like grass, they soon fade away. Like spring flowers, they soon wither. Trust in the Lord and do good. Then you will live safely in the land and prosper. Take delight in the Lord, and he will give you your heart's desires." (NLT)

Little did I know then how much that moment was going to change me. I had read the passage before. I even memorized the first part of it, but there are some things that you don't ascribe to yourself or your circumstances. There's a difference between memorizing Scripture and having a revelation from Scripture.

That was a revelation. I'd heard it before, the Holy Spirit reminded me of it, and when I looked it up, I knew it was for me.

Furthermore, I was reminded of what I saw my mother do often as I grew up—bringing home kids from the children's home or doing something kind for kids with special needs. It wasn't just people, either. We had a three-legged cat, and one time I saw my mother jump into a choppy lake in a storm just to rescue a squirrel that had fallen into the water after being blown out of a tree. My mom had some unspoken criteria that said something had to be wrong with you before she would love you. She certainly had her problems, especially with alcohol. But mom was a beautiful, artistic, talented individual who willingly chose to associate with those who were definitely less fortunate than she was. It was a lesson that had lived on with me beyond her death, and still does today.

In prison, I was living in a world full of despicable people who were just like that squirrel and three-legged cat. They were wounded animals, many of which had behaved like animals or worse. Yet I knew going forward that I was going to have to start looking for the good in them and trust the Lord to deal with the rest. I wasn't condoning their crimes. But I was going to have to take this chance to again change the way I thought about certain people—and how I acted toward them.

Freddy Mims was an inmate who was definitely on the MR side of things (I know today the proper term is "intellectually disabled"). He was kind of slow, big, and drooled a little bit. People made fun of him all the time. Prompted by the Holy Spirit and remembrance of my mother, I ended up befriending Freddy. More than that, I started telling everyone, "This is my twin, Freddy," when we were actually complete opposites. But it was a first, vital step for me to stop being so arrogant. I had this pompous air of confidence about myself. I shut almost everybody out because of how I was trying to live—but in doing so, I was shutting out the people that the Lord was putting in my path to help, care for, and make an impact in their lives.

I was learning how to be a better human being, and my next experience would take it to a whole other level.

~~~~

The realization came one day when I thought about lifers—people who are serving a life sentence. The big question in prison is, "How many years have you got?" Someone might respond, "I've got 10 years," or "I've got 20." You ask a lifer that question when you don't know they are a lifer, and they'll say, "I have alphabets. I have a life sentence. There is no number."

L-I-F-E-R.

I began to understand that I was meeting people that probably no one else in the world would ever be able to meet. These guys were never getting out, and some of them had already been locked up for decades. They were always a group unto themselves, and, for the most part, they weren't really tolerant of too many others.

So, how in the world I ever became friends with Dennis Washington was pretty amazing. Over the years, and later to his wife, I described us this way: "I'm young, and he's old. I'm smiling all the time, and he's grumpy. I'm white, and he's black. I like the Saints, and he likes the Cowboys." Most importantly, I added, "I was getting out one day, and unless a miracle happened, he was going to die in prison. It just wasn't going to be alone."

Dennis and I didn't start out being friends. Like all the lifers, he always seemed to be angry. But Dennis was a baker in the kitchen, so he and I crossed paths regularly. He came to me almost every morning and placed an order, usually for the nurses in the infirmary. That kind of thing happened all the time. If someone had access to the back of the kitchen where I was, they'd request two or three breakfasts and then take them to people all over the prison. Sometimes all it seemed I was doing was cooking, cooking, cooking.

One particular day, my patience was wearing real thin when Dennis showed up to make his request for the nurses. "Do you think, by taking them breakfast, you're going to get laid for some eggs and sausage?" I asked.

It was crass—and his response punched me right in the throat.

"Man, don't you know I have a life sentence? I'm going to die in this place. I just hope that when I'm over there dying that they remember my kindness and that they take care of me."

I felt like a worm. All I could think to say was, "How many breakfasts do you need?"

John would always tell people this about me, "Listen, this is what I know about Doug. Doug is gonna mess up. He's gonna say something he's not supposed to. He gonna do something he's not supposed to do. But the Holy Spirit is gonna speak to him, and he is gonna make an adjustment every single time. He's not gonna stay stuck in it."

Yep, I felt like such a jerk, but Dennis said what I needed to hear. His reality was just that. He was going to die in prison, and that realization changed how I felt about Dennis from that day forward.

Dennis stayed a cranky old fart—but what he now had was me loving that cranky old fart. I made a point every day to find him and make him talk with me. He didn't like it one bit, but I never gave up.

One thing that people leaving prison are notorious for doing is promising to write and send money to the friends they left behind, then rarely following through on that promise. But I committed to myself that when I left, I *was* going to write and send money to Dennis, and that as long as he was alive, I'd be there for him.

I didn't tell his grumpy self that. I wanted it to be a surprise that kept on going. Besides, if I'd have told him anything, he probably would've said something grumpy back at me.

By the time I did leave the prison to transition into a work release program, I'd learned so much about Dennis. I'd decided that he was a really great man who did something he really regretted. There is no justification, I suppose, for first degree murder, but I can say he made a mistake. It was a stupid thing he did in an angry situation that could have been avoided, a decision that ended up costing Dennis everything.

Dennis was mad at himself. He was definitely mad at God. Dennis hardly had anybody visit him. He always talked about his son and grandkids, as well as his ex-wife and his momma and all the people he loved and missed. He tried to send them stuff with the little bit of money he made as a lifer, 15 or 20 cents an hour for a 40-hour week of work. Dennis worried about his boy who, just like I had, was selling and doing drugs. Any daddy was going to worry about his son. I don't think Dennis saw him at all in the eight years I was there.

Before I left, Dennis opened up his heart and let me, this young, smiling, happy white boy, into his world. He had started to teach some of the younger guys coming in ways that they could avoid getting a life sentence. I later met his wife, son, daughter-in-law, and grandkids. They loved Dennis as best they knew how. God knows, so did I.

After I began serving work release, I stayed true to my word. I wrote and sent money to Dennis as often as I could. I even tried to get the people that I worked for in the prison to let me visit Dennis. They shot me down for the first four years, but I didn't quit. I reached out to some folks that I had favor with, they went to the top, and they eventually secured permission for me to visit him at the prison. That was amazing in and of itself, in that since I was on parole, I was legally exempt from going back into the prison because of my status and the security risk. But they made an exception for me.

Every three months, Dennis was allowed to have a picnic with a special visitor. Normally, it would be outdoors somewhere in the prison yard, but because I was a convicted felon, we had to do our picnics indoors in the visitation room. That didn't dissuade us, though. I cooked and brought in whatever he wanted to eat: steak, shrimp, pot pies. I had people bake cakes. We had so much food. Each time, we spent three hours together talking and eating and shooting the bull, all the while getting to know each other on a different level.

It was a Tuesday night in April 2017 when Dennis called me after he'd been to the infirmary. "They told me I've got this spot on my lung. They think it's cancer. I have to go back in a couple of weeks."

"Buddy, we are gonna get through this," I told him, adding that I was going to begin the long process of finding out what I needed to do to request and secure a medical furlough for Dennis. I began working with Major Matthews, who oversaw the prison's security departments and had been so kind to me when I was incarcerated, to see what could be done. Next, I talked to my wife about the situation. In early May, Kristin and I went together to visit Dennis.

As we were pulling up to the prison, she pointed off to the right. "What is that over there?" It was a cemetery. I answered, "That is where you get buried when you don't have family."

She looked at me and said, "We are not letting Dennis get buried in there."

"No," I said, "we most definitely are not." We even committed that we'd bring him to our home to live out his final days if the medical furlough allowed us to do so.

I had one more visit with Dennis in late June. It was just the two of us, and I brought along all of his favorite foods for our picnic, including his beloved German Chocolate cake. But he was so sick he could barely even eat. I could tell he was losing weight, too.

In July, Dennis called me to say his cancer was getting worse and that he didn't have much time to live. Determined, I again called the major to see where we stood with the furlough. A process I had hoped would only take a few weeks to accomplish still hadn't been resolved.

"Look, I'm calling about Dennis—"

She interrupted. "Yeah, we can talk about that, but we are in lockdown. There's an escape going on at this time."

When the situation was over, I tried to contact Major Matthews again, but she wasn't available. Frustrated, I waited for a response.

Then, on August 5, I got a voice message at 4:00 in the morning from a hospital near the prison. Fearing the worst,

I called, and they told me I'd been contacted because I was listed as the emergency contact and next of kin.

Dennis had passed away. The cancer had eaten him up. My friend did not end up in that cemetery. Kristin and I paid for all the expenses of his cremation and funeral service. It was held at a little church in Ruston, Louisiana, which was his hometown and where his family lived.

I did his eulogy, the only white person in the building beside my family. I told everyone that the Dennis they knew was not the Dennis I knew. I spoke for 45 minutes, sharing a message about finding hope in the defining moments of our lives. When it was over, there was not a dry eye in that place.

His ex-wife came up to me afterward. "Dennis was a good man. I sent him divorce papers, and he never would sign them."

I said, "That sounds like Dennis."

I have dedicated this book to Dennis. He thought he would just live out the life he had left, leave the earth, and nobody would ever know him or remember him. I do not want his legacy to die with him. It's the least I can do.

I really miss Dennis. It's been a few years since the last time I was with my buddy, but it still feels like it was yesterday.

~~~~

The work release that formally ended my time behind bars happened in July 2008. By then, John Skipworth and I were more than best friends. We'd become like brothers. The two of us had experienced so many things in the six years we were behind bars together. Having someone in prison who I trusted with my life, spiritually as well as physically, was more valuable than I could've ever imagined.

As we did things together, I realized that both of us had strong personalities and different leadership skills, so much so that I was willing to let my friend take the lead. I didn't want us to possibly damage a great friendship by being in needless conflict.

For example, John and I had the chance to work together on a project to create a baseball field in the prison yard. When I asked him to help me cut out the grid for the field, we had two very strong opinions about how to go about it. I wanted it to be done one way. He thought it would be best accomplished another way. When the same thing happened on other occasions, I knew that, for the sake of the friendship, somebody was going to have to take a step back. We didn't need to have two A-dogs.

I didn't diminish who I was, but I allowed him to be who he was, and we didn't have any challenges after that. It helped me learn that things that are important to me aren't nearly as important as having a friend.

By then, John and I had recognized that we had a call from God on our lives to do some great things, but we also knew it was going to be in separate areas. John was completing his theological studies to become a pastor (people either called him "Skip" or "Preacher"). I would kid around with him and say, "You are gonna preach, and I am gonna pass the plate." I thought then that I might be involved in doing something with John inside a church, but, in all honesty, I really had no clue exactly what my calling was at that time.

I remember sitting on the side of my bunk one day. Everybody was talking about what they did, and how some of them thought the lifestyle they'd lived was fun. I looked around at our cell block. "If this is the end result of fun," I said, "then I don't want it." We then started discussing what we were going to do when we got out, and where we wanted to work. They knew I'd had a business outside of prison and that I could run a business inside of prison.

"What about you, Doug?" someone asked.

"I don't know, but I'll say this. If I have to flip burgers at McDonald's, I'll do it."

John and I did assume that whatever it was we ended up doing, we'd surely be going to the same place. Why separate us as we transitioned into the next phase of our journey?

I just *knew* we'd be together. I didn't see any reason why we wouldn't.

Therefore, we were both disappointed when we found out I was going to south Louisiana while he was staying in the northern part of the state. When I asked the classification officer, the person who made recommendations about prisoner assignment, about it, her response surprised me.

"There is no way the two of you are going to the same place. You are too smart, too good looking, and too close." Then, with brutal honesty, she added, "I don't think either one of you are going to make it separately, and you certainly won't if you're together."

"Well, you don't know my friend," I told her in a not-so-polite way, "and there is no way John Skipworth or myself are ever coming back to prison once we leave!"

She shook her head. "We will see," she said.

"We certainly will," I responded.

John and I left a couple of weeks apart from each other. He went to the City of Faith in Monroe while I was assigned to the Lafourche Parish Work Release southwest of New Orleans along the Gulf of Mexico. It was kind of a miracle how I got transferred down there and when it happened: a combination of a statute change that made me eligible for work release a full year earlier than expected, and the nosiness of a different classifications officer who otherwise would likely have never noticed the statute revision and how it applied to my sentence. Despite being separated from John, I was going to get a chance to get a job offshore, which was everyone's dream in prison.

After all, I thought, *why not me!*

Change was coming. I had no clue yet as to its extent, but I did know I was more motivated than ever to prove people, like that classification officer, wrong.

I *was* going to stay out of prison, and I was also going to stay close with my best friend, even if it did have to be a long-distance relationship.

~~~~~

When it was all said and done, those seven years inside Forcht-Wade Correctional Center really did serve me. Granted, there were some long days, struggling with depression and ruminating about everything happening on the outside that I couldn't control. I remember one time when I spoke to my father on the phone. I told him, "It's just so easy to go to prison." I could almost hear him smile. "Son," he replied, "it's not easy to go to prison. Do you realize how long you've been doing what you've been doing, all the rules and laws you've been breaking. As a matter of fact, you worked really hard to get in prison." That thought has never left me. I'd surely had plenty of opportunities to not end up behind bars.

But then came all the interventions by the Lord, the experiences I had with Him, and the changes of perspective and behavior that it caused.

Despite everything that had happened in my past, I chose to do what I had to do. I learned that when you have to do something, you don't really have a choice *whether* you do it or not, but you do have a choice *how* to do it. I just did the right thing: I did my own thing, stayed away from trouble, served my sentence, and spent time with the Lord. God protected me the entire time.

I also discovered how to gain control of my emotions. I applied for pardon hearings and risk reviews so many times, only to continue to be denied. A psychologist for the prison (she later became the warden) had a chance to watch me grow and develop while I was in prison. Regarding all the denials, she later told me, "I never, ever saw you lose your character. Usually when that happens to people in prison, they end up crashing out. They get in trouble, get rebellious, or go to solitary. You never did that. You just kept pushing forward with your head held high. That is not normally what you see."

I discovered I had to keep myself really motivated, and I did.

I didn't want to just go through the motions. I wanted to do something. Be someone.

Yes, the time behind bars did serve me.

Question was, what was going to happen once I was out this time?

That's me, chilling in the shade on the beach in Galveston, TX. I was one year old.

Dad holding Mark, Penny hugging mom, and me at four years of age at My Ma's house in Dallas, TX. My suit was the best!

With Mark at My Ma's house when I was four years old. I loved that Acapulco t-shirt with the sailfish.

A childhood Christmas at My Ma's house. (L to R): My Ma, mom, and me with my Uncle Carlton looking down on me. Dad is standing in the background, and my Grandpa Harry is in the chair. We eventually lived in that home with My Ma.

With Mark (I'm on the left) outside The Alamo in 1978. I was seven years old.

Outside Aunt Debbie's house in San Antonio, TX. I was in fourth grade.

Hanging out at Aunt Debbie's house. I was nine years old.

(L to R): Mark, mom, Aunt Debbie (seated) with her baby daughter, My Ma, and me at 11 years of age. It was Christmas at Aunt Debbie's house.

Hitting the skins at Uncle Carlton's music studio in Dallas, TX with mom looking on. I'm 11 years old.

My oldest daughter when she was six years old.

The last location of Tiger Tan in 2001.

My stepmom, dad, and me at Christmas in Slidell, LA right before I went to prison.

With Mark (I'm the fella in the one-piece jumpsuit) at the Lasalle Parish Correctional Center, August 2002.

Uncle Carlton and Aunt Debbie in 2003 while I was incarcerated.

One of the photos sent to me while I was in prison of Penny in an equestrian competition on a horse she trained and raised.

At the Forcht-Wade visiting shed at Christmas 2004 with Amy holding her daughter, Lauren, her husband, Bill, and Mark.

At the Forcht-Wade visiting shed with my stepmom and dad, Christmas 2004.

With my godsend, John Skipworth, in prison, 2005.

At Forcht-Wade in 2005 with dad and Mark at the visiting shed.

With Captain Dan at the Gulf of Mexico, Fall 2008.

Pumping it up on the deck barge during my offshore work release.

Kristin posing next to the Ouachita River in downtown Monroe, LA. This is one week after our first date.

"Aw, you're so pretty! Let me take a picture." Kristin in the driveway at her mother's house.

Kristin just before our wedding ceremony, Gulf Shores, AL, October 20, 2010.

Kristin ready to walk down the sandy aisle. Our wedding day in Gulf Shores.

The most blessed man alive! Our wedding day in Gulf Shores.

A perfect sunset for a perfect moment. Our wedding day in Gulf Shores.

The Blonde Bomber and the girl with the smile that would stop the Rapture! With Kristin at a restaurant.

With John holding our first born children, June 2013. Just another way our lives have been in sync. Doesn't baby Michael look great?

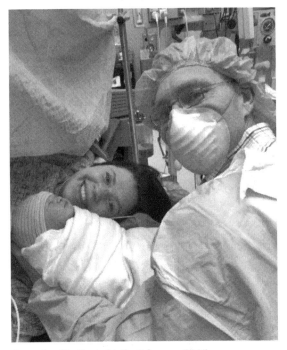

Just after Hadley's birth, February 2015.

*Goofing off with the kids in our backyard, November
2015. Michael is almost three, and Hadley is nine
months old. No, I didn't pick out our clothes!*

*With Kristin for a surprise renewal of our wedding
vows, Gulf Shores, August 2016.*

Visiting Dennis Washington at Forcht-Wade in 2015.

My last Christmas visit with Dennis in 2016.

The last time I visited Dennis, June 2017.

A commemorative plaque in tribute to my precious friend.

Getting ready to skydive with Penny, November 2017 in Slidell.

All dressed up for a costume party fundraising event, March 2019.

Hadley and Michael at Dixie Youth Baseball, March 2019.

Letting Michael have a turn at the wheel (sort of) on Bayou Lacombe, March 2019.

Enjoying time together at Lake Pontchartrain near New Orleans, LA, March 2019.

Our happy family at Lake Pontchartrain, March 2019. Michael is seven and Hadley is five.

The day Mark got married, May 2019. I can't believe he didn't want a kiss!

She did it! Kristin's graduation day from college, May 2019.

Worshipping God at one of our nights of encounter at New Day, Fall 2019. That's Michael in the foreground.

With Hadley in her catcher's gear, April 2021.

With Hadley on the soccer field with her participation trophy, the first year I coached her. April 2021.

With Michael in front of the soccer goal with the championship runners-up trophy, my third year of coaching him. April 2021.

CHAPTER SIX

—

FREE AT LAST—OR WAS I?

I WAS STILL AN INMATE, but I was in the work release program, so surely that was a step in the right direction.

Now, I just had to figure out how to get a job offshore. Once I did that, I knew I'd feel just a bit freer than I really was.

Offshore employment was really *the* dream job for a prisoner on work release. It paid good money, usually $125 or $150 a day. Plus, there were no guards or security officers supervising you when working offshore. It was more like you weren't in prison at all, and you were one step closer to physical freedom.

I was willing to do whatever it took to work offshore. Problem was, I didn't have any practical experience, at least not anything I could brag about. They were looking for an experienced deckhand, someone who had worked on the sea on a crew boat, tugboat, or a rig. I didn't have any of that. There was also a nationwide economic recession going on in 2008.

Therefore, I was certainly glad when I finally found a job—and even more thankful when I got two.

I split my time between working 12-hour shifts as a laborer in the shipyards and 13-hour stints as a hopper on the trash truck, leaping on and off the truck hauling garbage. Both paid $8.00 an hour, only 75 cents above minimum wage, but I didn't care. I didn't have a problem with hard labor, and I'd spent the past seven-and-a-half years working for free, so to me it was an 800 percent increase in pay.

The work release center was a medium security facility with five dorms housing up to 40 men each, offices, a day room, and a dining area. It wasn't completely fenced off, and the main highway was a hundred or so yards from the front entrance of the parking lot. It took two hours each way to get to and from the center and the shipyards, where I painted United States Coast Guard cutters, grinded metal, and assisted crane operators who were loading and securing cargo. One of the worst tasks was cleaning out the oil tanks. I had to stand three feet deep in guck that smelled like sulfur and shovel it all out. It was a lot of grunt work wearing a hard hat, steel toe boots, and safety goggles in south Louisiana in the summer. That's what I did Monday-Friday, with the weekends spent on trash detail.

My first day as a garbage man, about a week into my work release, was quite interesting. That morning, the scripture I read from the Bible was Colossians 3:23. "Whatever you do, work at it with all your heart, as working for the Lord, not for human masters." With that directive in my mind and heart, I put that same smile on my face that I'd first discovered back in jail and went to work.

As I stood at the end of the road outside the work release facility waiting for the garbage truck to pick me up, the driver, a lady, slowed down, but seemed reluctant to stop. She was almost past me when she finally braked to a halt. She leaned her head out the driver's side window.

"Who are you?" she asked. She looked like she didn't see too many white guys out there, and certainly no one with a big smile on their face. I could imagine her thinking, *Is this really who they sent out here to work?*

I kept my response pretty literal. "I'm Doug Pollock, and I'm waiting for the garbage truck."

She shook her head. I was probably a little too chipper for her taste. "Well, you must never have done the garbage truck job before because no one else I've ever picked up had a smile as big as yours!" She motioned for me to get in, and when I climbed in the cab, there was another worker there with her. I held out my hand. "Hi! I'm Doug Pollock," I repeated, "and I'll be working with you today."

As I shook hands with the co-worker, the driver leaned over to the other person. "We will see if he is still smiling at the end of the day."

That made me grin even bigger.

In south Louisiana, July and August are hot, very hot, and every afternoon, it rains at least once and gets hotter still. Not only that, but most everyone in south Louisiana drinks beer and eats seafood. You can only imagine what the heat and humidity do to that combination of waste in a garbage bin. Old seafood, stale beer, and ants. It's a great mix.

After that initial long day of hopping, I was good and broke in by the end of the shift. As the driver was taking me back to the work release facility, she said, "I don't know who you are or where you came from, but I've never seen anyone work so hard and smile all day like you have. I need you back on my truck tomorrow."

I told her about the verse I'd read that morning and how I felt I'd just got an 800 percent raise. I then explained my conviction that whether I made $8.00 or $80.00 an hour, I had to put in my best effort.

"But what about that smile of yours?" she asked as we got to my stop and I began climbing down from the cab.

"Well, in my mind, the best way to get a promotion is this. If I can smile and do this job, someone higher up will notice and wonder what's wrong with me. When they ask, that'll be my chance." Then I added, "I'll be waiting for you tomorrow."

After working on her truck for a couple of weekends, I was majorly disappointed when I got up Monday morning and saw that my name wasn't on the list to go out and work in the shipyards. *Did I do something wrong?* I was concerned, but with nothing else to do at that moment, I laid back down to go to sleep until a guard tapped on the top of my bunk.

"The captain wants to see you," she said. This guard had always had a friendly disposition, and she sounded excited.

"What for?" I asked groggily.

"I think it's about an offshore job," she replied.

I jumped up as fast as I could. Captain Zeringue was the head guy in charge of offshore assignments. I got dressed, walked across to the building housing the offices, and he met me at the door to his office.

"Have you ever worked offshore?" he asked. He sounded more curious than skeptical.

Here's my chance, I thought. "No, but I grew up on the water." I hoped my reply would stretch things out a bit. It was surely better than a straight out "no."

"Can you tie off a boat?"

"I can—but it was a small boat." I flashed back to the first time I was ever on a boat. I was six years old, and our family had a red fishing boat. I have no idea why I thought back to that specific moment. I lost my fishing pole that day.

"I'm not sure why I'm talking to you about this job," he admitted, "but I had them keep you in this morning."

I've never said, "I can't do it." I had been praying and believing for this a long time. I needed to convince Captain Zeringue and assure him that he could fit the square peg in the round hole. Trying to sound confident, not desperate, I said, "If you'll just let me go for the interview, I know I can get the job. I'll be the best worker you ever had, and I won't give you a black eye if you trust me."

I had never said that term before, though I knew it reflected how others typically felt about those in prison.

They don't believe them. I wanted the captain to know he could trust me and that I wouldn't let him down.

I guess I was convincing enough. "Okay, Doug. I'll send you over, but I still don't know why—except that I've seen you every morning getting on that garbage truck with a smile, and there's one still there when you get off."

I had no idea he'd been watching me.

It's important to remember that others are paying attention to us, so what we do and how we go about doing it matters.

I spoke with Captain Zeringue at 7:00 a.m. I was on my way to Reeves Boat Company in nearby Houma, Louisiana by 8:00, took my physical by 9:30, and had the results of the physical before lunch. I passed, I was hired, and I went out on the boat the next day. I was on Cloud Nine—and I stayed there all week as I worked on a crew boat that serviced oil rigs on the Gulf. I was supposed to have a rotating schedule where I'd be out for a week and then back in for the next week—but after that initial shift, I was able to convince the folks at Reeves that they didn't need to hire anyone else for the next off week.

I ended up being out on the boat for the next five months. It was such freedom that, to some extent, I actually forgot I was still a prisoner.

I did a lot during that time, taking people in and out during crew changes and servicing the needs of the rig. I learned how to dock a big boat and navigate with the tide. When I had any free moments, I lifted weights, and I jumped rope so much I broke most of them in half. Every time we went to shore, I ran the levees. I maintained my physical exercise, and it was my only time to be away from others.

I met a bunch of people, though, and they could see I stayed active and busy. I cleaned our boat all the time, and I often painted the deck. It was amazing how many coats of paint I could put on top of other layers of paint. My work ethic was obvious, and it was that ethic that made people ask questions and want to get to know me.

One thing I didn't do was run around quoting this Bible verse or that. I was trying to live out what I believed, just as I had for so long in prison. On the most part, my crewmates would work seven or 14 days, make their money, go in for a week and party, then return to do their job all over again. The majority were a rough bunch. They lived the lifestyle I used to live—but that was what drew me to them. I knew I could relate to them, but they needed to first see who I was, then know who I was, before I thought they could know what I believed about God.

That said, there was a black guy from Mississippi, Charles Ealy, who was probably in his mid-twenties. He was a rigger, the person on the ground who held the lines holding cargo being hauled by a crane to make sure that cargo stayed safe and secure as it was moved. He and I spoke to one another a lot—and he was the one who actually got me to start doing a Bible study each week for many of the rig hands. Charles would sit in the cabin of the boat, see me reading the Bible or my study books, and it drew his interest. He asked if I'd be interested in doing a Bible study with him and some of the other crew members, and I told him I'd be glad to.

We had to fit in the studies as we went, depending on our responsibilities for that week, and I was like the friendly greeter at church, quickly forming relationships with those who attended. I wanted to show them how I got out of the lifestyle I used to be in, and I used verses that were (and still are) instrumental to me.

The first was Ephesians 1:16-20. It read, "I have not stopped giving thanks for you, remembering you in my prayers. I keep asking that the God of our Lord Jesus Christ, the glorious Father, may give you the Spirit of wisdom and revelation, so that you may know him better. I pray that the eyes of your heart may be enlightened in order that you may know the hope to which he has called you, the riches of his glorious inheritance in his holy people, and his incomparably great power for us who believe. That power is the same as the mighty strength he exerted when he raised Christ from the dead." I had lived a life of powerlessness to addiction and lust, so if I could ever fully realize that kind of power—resurrection power—in my life, I knew I could overcome temptation. I just had to believe it.

The other was from Ephesians 3:16-18. "I pray that out of his glorious riches he may strengthen you with power through his Spirit in your inner being, so that Christ may dwell in your hearts through faith. And I pray that you, being rooted and established in love, may have power, together with all the Lord's holy people, to grasp how wide and long and high and deep is the love of Christ."

Those two passages of Scripture were foundational when I thought about how I had been so powerless over my addictions, yet there was greater power available to me through God. I led the men through discussions of things that were going on in their lives, and I used those two passages to introduce them to the Word of God. As far as what we studied, it was usually some sort of devotional that I had read that day or something else I was studying. It was an informal process, and as questions came up, we discussed them.

The captain, Dan Burgett (who I called Uncle Dan), had the reputation of being a hard, old salty dog, but I discovered that Uncle Dan was a good man with a kind spirit who just wanted things done a certain way. Every morning, he'd see me get up and read my Bible. He never said anything. He just sat there while he had coffee and watched me. He knew it was an important part of my life.

Uncle Dan was kind of like a different version of Dennis. I heard what people thought of him and what they believed about him, but I chose to see him differently, hoping to discover who he really was behind the hard exterior. Uncle Dan taught me about the ocean, the current, how to look for weather signs, and what those signs meant. In return, I worked hard and kept the boat just like he wanted.

When the seasons began to change and the winds blew in from the north, we'd often head inshore to tie up instead of staying out there to ride out the rough waves. It was normally just for the night before we had to go back out. It was rare to be tied up for 24 hours or longer. There were always two boats and three crews at any one time, and the captains rotated every week. On my boat, I was either working under Uncle Dan or another captain, a big, jolly younger guy named Sandy. The other boat's captains were named Michael and Roy, and Roy and one of his deckhands usually went out to play billiards and drink when we were tied up onshore. They often asked me to join them.

At first, I didn't go, but I eventually gave in. Shooting pool was something that made me comfortable—and I told myself I could do that, but I wasn't going to drink, no matter how much they asked me to do so. It was no big deal.

Then, one night, I had a Corona, the beer I primarily drank before I went to prison. After that first one? Well, I went ahead and tried every new beer and liquor that had come out the past eight years. I even shot some tequila. The whole time I was thinking to myself, *Man, I hope I don't get sick. I haven't had liquor in me in forever.*

I never did get sick, and if anything, that bothered me. I picked up right where I left off. I didn't miss a beat, and I stayed out all night long with them.

The next day, I woke up in the bridge. I was laying on a mat atop a bench the size of a twin bed that's much like a little crow's nest, a cubby place next to the back window of the bridge, where I apparently found a place to sleep. When I came to, it was 10 o'clock in the morning. I hadn't slept in that late in I don't know how long.

I felt horrible. Nasty. Dirty.

I smelled like a bar.

I had betrayed myself.

~~~~~

I had stayed in touch with John, talking with him several times each week on the contraband cellphone my dad had sent me (technically, as a prisoner, I still wasn't supposed to have my own phone) and that I used to call him, my step-mom, and Mark when I was offshore. John would tell me all about what he was doing in Monroe, and I'd tell him all about what I was doing in the Gulf. Every time we spoke, he'd insist that I needed to come to Monroe, like I could just up and move there. He maintained he could get me there if I wanted to come, and he described the privileges he had, including being able to go to church.

I thought I was so much more free because I was out on the Gulf, and I kept telling him that I had a plan to get my captain's license so I could earn $600 a day driving a boat. While John never outright said my idea was crazy, I knew he thought it was. He was my best friend, he knew me well, and he knew what he felt the Lord wanted me to achieve—and it wasn't captaining a boat. But at that time, I was thinking, *I have a chance to rebuild my life, but I can't rebuild it on hope and faith alone. I need money, good money.* Before I went to prison, whether it was from the drugs or my businesses, I always had the money to do what I wanted to do. So, I was trying to figure out how to get back to where I was finan-cially as fast as I possibly could, and I reasoned $600 a day as a boat captain would be a pretty good start.

Of course, I didn't tell John that I'd started drinking again. I assumed I already knew how he'd feel about it, and I just didn't want to hear him say it.

Meanwhile, every chance we had to come inshore, I kept tagging along with the other captain and his mate so I could play pool when really, I was going so that I could drink. All kinds of new brews and spirits had come out since I'd first gone to prison, and I just had to try them all, right?

Truth was the addict in me hadn't gone away. It was just as persistent as it was before I was incarcerated. In fact, during one outing around Halloween, the captain of the other boat and his deckhand were planning on getting some Ecstasy and kept asking me if I wanted some. They were never able to get the drug, but I can tell you this: if they had, I don't know what I would have done. To this day, I'm so glad whatever they had planned fell through because I was so tempted.

I don't believe I would have done it, but I could have. That's the scary part.

As far as God was concerned, I was praying to Him for help, but it was the typical, "Lord, I am so sorry, forgive me, and I promise I won't do this again" sort of prayer. It was more about Him taking it away than about helping me have the strength and willpower to say no.

It was crazy. In prison, I had spent over seven years learning how to follow the rules and regulations and stay within the lines. Outside of prison, I had a different sense of freedom. I had to discover not what the rules were, but *who I was*. It was one of the first opportunities where I really had to start realizing the power that those scriptures from Ephesians were talking about in relation to who I was in Him. Freedom, real freedom, was having the ability to do anything in the world that I wanted, good or bad, right or wrong—but always choosing the right thing based on the true and authentic version of me in Him and Him in me.

In the end, I made a total of five trips to "play pool" before I had another mirror encounter. This one came at 5:00 a.m. at a bar in Venice, Louisiana. Venice is located on the tip of the Louisiana boot and is about as far south as you can get in the United States aside from Texas or Florida. We called it the bottom of the world—and that adequately described the bathroom I walked into at the bar. Shabby and smoky, it reeked of urine and was illuminated by one yellow, dim bulb hanging from the ceiling. Still, it had just enough lumens for me to see what I looked like in the small, square mirror after I closed the door.

I couldn't believe it. My eyes were red and puffy. My face was splotchy, and my cheeks were flushed.

Yet it was what I viewed beyond the reflection—the person I was inside—that really got me.

Sometimes you can forget who you are, but you never forget who you're not. At that moment, I realized just how far back I had slipped since leaving Forcht-Wade and how far out of alignment I was mentally, emotionally, and spiritually since I began my work release.

I looked right into my own eyes. "I know I didn't spend the last seven years becoming the person I am only to let this guy back into the picture. I haven't come this far only to go back to where I started."

I saw a drunk in that dingy mirror—but I chose to believe that what I saw was not really who I was.

That was the last time I ever got drunk.

~~~~

The very next day, I called John.

"Man, I messed up. I got drunk. I got drunk a few times."

We had a long conversation, and like the great friend he was, John didn't shame me or tell me how stupid I was. All he did was ask, "Well, what are you going to do?"

Again, I took the literal approach. "Obviously, I am not going to keep getting drunk."

"That's good," he replied, "but what about coming here with me? I can get you up here."

"What kind of job can I get there," I countered. "I'm making good money now."

His reply wasn't a surprise. "We've spent all these years in prison living on faith. We have seen God do things in our seven years that people would never see God do in their whole life, all because of what we chose to believe. You can't ask questions that are going to make you doubt. You're just going to have to come in faith and find out."

I told John that I needed to pray about it, and I'd get back to him.

For the next 10 days, I kept asking God to give me a sign or a word, anything that would tell me what I needed to do. No matter what I saw and heard, there was nothing giving me any idea I was supposed to go to Monroe. Then came the afternoon I was sitting on the back of the boat listening to a message by Dr. Jerry Savelle, and I asked the Lord to give me a sign like letting a bunch of seagulls land on the deck. At that point, I probably would've considered some seagull poop on the deck a sign from the Lord, but I didn't even get that.

About 55 minutes into the hour-long message, I heard Dr. Savelle mention how God asked Abraham to go to into the land that he would later receive as his inheritance. "Now Abraham didn't ask God what kind of a job he was going to have," Savelle said. "The Bible just says he obeyed and went."

There it was, and I didn't even need a seagull's bodily function to hammer it home.

Right there and then, I knew I needed to go.

I called John, told him what happened, and declared that I was ready for my next journey to start. "Make it happen," I told him.

Five days later, we were tied up just off the rig, and I was cleaning the boat when Uncle Dan hollered at me from across the deck. "You got a phone call!"

It had come directly to him, not to my contraband cell. My heart skipped a beat. *What in the world could that be about?*

I went over to Uncle Dan. "Who is it?"

He handed me the phone. "It's Captain Zeringue."

I had the same feeling as when my parole officer would show up at my house unannounced, or when I'd taken a drug test and wondered if it was going to come back clean. *This can't be good. I know I went to the bar a few times. Did someone see me or report me?*

I stood on the front part of the boat, right above the ship's galley, as I took the call.

Captain Zeringue got right to the point. "I got a phone call today from some place in Monroe, Louisiana called City of Faith. They told me that you wanted to be transferred. Is that true?"

"Yes, sir, it is," I said, and I paused, probably for just a few seconds, but it seemed like forever. Then I finished, "But not right now."

Suddenly, despite what I had told John, I got cold feet. "I want to work on getting my captain's license first. I only need 120 more hours out here, and I can take my test."

"Well, then," Captain Zeringue said with what sounded like condescending disbelief, "I don't want to hear anything else about this City of Faith," and he hung up the phone.

I could only imagine how upset he probably was, getting a call from some other place saying I wanted a transfer. Yet he didn't ask me how it had happened or why. All he wanted to do was shut it down—and I let him.

Instantly, I knew I had messed up. I was hesitant, maybe even scared. It was like everything was going too fast, and I had to slam on the brakes. In this situation, I had not only become content with where I was, but I was settling, even compromising. Because I had been in such a bad place for such a long time, I had lost the ability to be dissatisfied in such a way that would make me pursue more and have a positive ambition and hunger for something better.

I couldn't believe what I had just done, so I called John right away on my cellphone to tell him I'd messed up. I just knew he could help me fix it.

Was I ever wrong!

"Dude, I did my part. I asked them to do you a favor, and now you've got to figure it out." He didn't sound angry. He was more disappointed than anything else.

It took me a couple of days to come up with a plan, but come up with one, I did. I wasn't sure how it was going to turn out. It consisted of me telling Uncle Dan I was going to have to quit my job, then calling the work release to tell them

I'd be coming ashore, before somehow meeting with Captain Zeringue to beg him to okay my transfer to City of Faith.

It sounded easy in theory, but as a prisoner (which, even if I didn't sometimes feel like it, I still was), I couldn't just up and quit my job, and getting back to the mainland from the Gulf of Mexico wasn't so easy, either.

I told Uncle Dan what I wanted to do, and it just so happened that the drilling company then decided to close down the rig we were assigned to, likely because of the economic recession. When that happened, we basically helped transport the rig back to where it is stored. That turn of events made it a bit easier for my plan to move along. When we got back in, I committed to dry dock the boat, meaning I helped bring it out of the water in the shipyard and scraped off the barnacles, painted the hull, and anything else necessary to prepare it for storage.

The events were negative, but I saw them as miraculous, in that it all worked in favor of what I was trying to do.

Once my work at the shipyard was completed, I returned to the Lafourche Parish Work Release program. It was a Friday afternoon, and I put in a request to speak with Captain Zeringue as soon as he'd see me.

The weekend passed, as did Monday, then Tuesday.

It wasn't until Wednesday that we finally got to talk.

Captain Zeringue, who I could only assume had delayed seeing me on purpose, wasn't interested in discussing any transfer. He only wanted to talk about one thing—and that was doing another job for him. He needed some painting done on the exterior of some U.S. Coast Guard cutters. The work was going to take 10 days. I agreed, but I told him that when I was done, I really wanted to talk about City of Faith.

I did the work, and after I was finished, Captain Zeringue called me in again.

His goal was to make me an offer I couldn't refuse.

"How much time do you have left in your sentence?" he asked.

"About 33 months," I told him.

"I have a job you could do for the next 33 months. After that, you could leave and never have to come back."

It was offshore like I had been doing, just on bigger rigs further out into the gulf.

It would take just under three years to complete. The pay was $50,000 a year.

Captain Zeringue looked at me. "Didn't you own your own business before?"

"Yes, sir, I did," I replied.

"Well, wouldn't you like to have enough money to start your own business again when you get out?"

"That would be nice," I said.

"I need a trustworthy person for this, and I feel like you're the one. But there's one condition. I don't want to hear anything else out of you about this City of Faith."

"Can I think about it" I asked.

He said yes. I began to walk out the door, and then I stopped and turned back to face Captain Zeringue.

"I know what I want to do—and I can't. All you have to offer me is a job that pays a lot of money, but on the inside, I'm dying. I am not growing spiritually. I just spent all that time in prison, and it's not so that I can go backwards. If the best you can do is offer me money, I'm not going to do it. I need to be in a place where my faith can grow."

"Man, you know you're crazy," he said incredulously. "We're in the middle of a recession."

"I came here with no job, and I got to this point," I replied. "If I go up there and I have to work on the back of a trash truck, just like I did down here, I'll do it with the biggest smile I could ever have."

He told me I was making a mistake.

I told him I was going to be a success story for him.

Early Monday morning, I was going to be on my way to City of Faith—but not before I got one more phone call Sunday night.

It was Captain Zeringue, calling from his home. "I just wanted to thank you," he told me sincerely. "We don't get guys like you that come through here that often. When you get one, you don't want to lose them. I guess I was just really trying to hold onto you. I want to wish you well. I appreciate you being a man of your word."

"It's really me that needs to thank you," I replied, "and I just want to remind you that I'm going to be a success story for you."

"You already are," he said.

That was the last time I ever spoke with Captain Zeringue. I believe that my faith in God challenged him to see inmates in a different light from that day forward.

CHAPTER SEVEN

I Finally Found It

THE SHERIFF'S DEPARTMENT transported me by van from the Lafourche Parish Work Release program north to City of Faith Prison Ministries in Monroe. Apparently, John established a strong relationship with the founder of City of Faith—so strong that when she asked him what he wanted for his birthday, he requested that she use her influence to get me transferred there.

It was unprecedented. But it worked.

When I arrived mid-morning, John was away, so I didn't get to see him until that afternoon. In the meantime, I checked in and looked around the place I'd heard so many great things about from John, and even from fellow inmates when I was at Forcht-Wade.

City of Faith consisted of five different houses on Jackson Street, and while it was a work release facility associated with the Louisiana Department of Corrections, it wasn't fenced in, and instead of guards, unarmed security personnel who were more like house managers kept an eye on everyone. While there were definite rules to follow, there was more of a sense of freedom about City of Faith than I'd experienced anywhere else before.

I was sent to the same house where John was staying, and it was large (each house was about 3,000 square feet or more in size). I was assigned a spot on a bunk bed in a room with 12 other men. Later, I'd be transitioned to a room with half that many people. My house, which provided shelter to about 30 men in all, was a two-story Victorian-style brick home that was in great shape for its age. City of Faith was certainly located in the "hood" of Monroe, but it was still a very nice place.

When I was reunited with John, it was as though we had never been apart, and he eagerly showed me around. I quickly discovered that what made City of Faith different was its faith-based programs and the people involved in them. They had a men's group that met every Tuesday night called "Real Talk" and was taught by a man named Ricky Banks. It was all about teaching men to be genuine and vulnerable, and I later saw that at the close of each session, each of us looked one another in the eyes and declared, "Brother, I love you."

That would prove to be just one example of how City of Faith had a caring, inviting atmosphere that was exemplified by its founder, Kathy Biedenharn, who first opened City of Faith in 1985.

My first night there, Miss Kathy took me, John, and another person to church and then out for dinner afterward. I learned she was a preacher who used to live a life of promiscuity. She understood all too well the barriers faced by people in prison as well as ex-cons, and she was a proponent for helping people overcome those obstacles. She was also a spitfire for the Lord. Part of City of Faith's vision, she said, was the recognition that life is a journey, and that everyone basically wants the same thing: to be recognized, to be cared for, and to have an opportunity to grow.

As I began taking part in the Bible study and church activities that City of Faith made available for those who wanted to attend, I could tell Miss Kathy had carefully selected a lot of the people who worked there who shared her heart for

God and for others. Through John, I was also introduced to Kevin and his wife, Barbara. At John's suggestion, I attended Kevin's men's group, my first time in such an environment where men just got together and talked about God's Word. I kept coming back, and eventually he asked me if I'd like to come to his house for Thanksgiving with his wife and family. I accepted, and that time with him and Barbara was pivotal. Their two adult children were there, along with their two grandchildren and Barbara's parents, and everyone instantly made me one of their own.

Kevin and I began meeting weekly, and he taught me how to be a Christian man and businessperson. Barbara treated me like a son and gave me motherly love different from anything I'd experienced before with my own mother or stepmom. I could call them up whenever I needed, and they became a lifeline for me as I grew accustomed to being in Monroe and at City of Faith. It was wonderful.

Like the work release in Lafourche Parish, City of Faith not only provided housing, but employment opportunities. The first six weeks I was there, I couldn't find anything steady. John had a close relationship with the pastor and his family at an area church, so every time there was a church get-together, we were there, and we spent time with the pastor's family. It was terrific to go to church and act like normal folks after all that time behind bars, and the pastor and his family were kind and caring. They were generous enough to let me mow grass and do other work at the church to put a few bucks in my pocket.

One of the really cool things about Miss Kathy was that she always asked, "What do you want to do?" and if I wanted to try it, she'd figure out a way to get me that job. She was always so kind and gracious to try to help me figure out what I wanted to do because she wanted me to be happy. Miss Kathy just had that type of heart.

I got a position as a personal trainer, but a couple of days in, after I told them I was in a halfway house and had been to prison, they suddenly didn't have a need for me anymore. That was kind of disheartening, but I tried not to let it get me down. I attempted selling cars, and although I could sell ice to an Eskimo, I thought it was boring.

Then I got a phone call from the pastor's daughter telling me that she'd heard McDonald's was hiring.

I immediately thought back to that conversation in prison when a bunch of us were talking about what we were going to do when we got out, and I had said, "If I have to flip burgers at McDonald's, I'll do it."

I didn't hesitate. I called, got an interview, and was hired—not just to flip burgers and work at the store on Bridge Street in West Monroe, Louisiana, but to go into their management training program.

I didn't lie on any of the applications. When it specifically asked, "Have you been convicted of a felony in the last five years?" I thought, *Well, it's been almost eight years, so I can safely answer "no" on that one.* But I didn't tell them I was at City of Faith or why I was there. I figured the last time I did that at the personal trainer job, it didn't go so well.

McDonald's training program was excellent, and after the first few weeks I knew they had plans for me. A lot of it was about food safety and related issues, but it really focused on customer service and the business side of running a restaurant. Considering my pre-prison experience at Tiger Tan, it was right up my alley. Before long, my manager, Brett, who was in the U.S. Army National Guard, had to go away for a couple of weeks of active duty, and he let me run the store.

I didn't do it perfectly, but I ended up making it work—which convinced me I needed to talk with him when he returned.

"Man, I probably need to tell you something," I started, and I shared everything about City of Faith and my background. "I just really wanted to let you know, because it looks like you all are wanting to put trust in me, and the last thing I want is for this to come out by happenstance instead of me coming to you."

He told his supervisor, Darren, and then his supervisor told the owner. I had heard that the owner was somebody who did not believe in God, so I was a bit worried—but when it was all said and done, my manager pulled me aside.

"The owner told Darren, 'Well, let's see what happens,'" he said.

I had made enough of a positive impression that they were going to give me a chance.

With Miss Kathy's blessing, I had been provided a bike to ride to and from work instead of having to be dropped of and picked up by the City of Faith van. I also enjoyed the sense of freedom that came from riding the bike. I always rode with my shirt off, and I wore a backpack that had my work clothes in it. It was hot outside, and I didn't want to go to work all sweaty. I'd always freshen up and change in the bathroom before starting my shift.

When I was working at the Bridge Street location, I rode right by a plain, non-descript brick building with dingy beige trim in downtown West Monroe. It had dark windows, an uninviting white front door and matching garage entrance, and three vehicles parked outside: a black Tahoe with tinted windows, a white Suburban, and a cool looking Jeep.

I used to think, *Man, is the Mafia in there? Are they dealing dope?*

Little did I know that inside that building was a man who, every time he saw me, would turn to his daughter and say, "Look! There goes the Blonde Bomber again."

I'd later discover just how significant that man's daughter was going to be in my life.

~~~~

After a couple of months at the Bridge Street store, I was transferred to a McDonald's on Thomas Road to continue my professional development. My duties there emphasized the development of some of the management tactics I needed in order to run my own store. This expanded on not only being familiar with anything that has to be done working at a McDonald's, but also being capable of doing it. I worked the grill. I worked the front. I worked the drive-thru window. It wasn't just so I could make sure the staff was doing everything the way they were supposed to, but because if the biscuit lady didn't come in that day, I had to know how to drop buttermilk biscuits and get them ready to serve.

It was also there that I learned a valuable lesson from Jerrald, who trained me at Thomas Road the day before I began work there. He pulled me aside and, speaking of my fellow employees, told me, "The impression that they have of you on the first day is the way that they will always see you. If you want them to know who you are and respect what you ask them to do, you get that on the first day."

Within three months, Darren approached me for another move—to actually manage a McDonald's in Ruston. The store was busy, located right by the Louisiana Tech University campus. Only problem was, it was 35 miles away down Interstate 20 from City of Faith, and I knew even the Blonde Bomber couldn't ride his bike that far.

"Man," I told Darren, "we need to go talk to Mister Ricky Banks."

By then, Ricky, Miss Kathy's executive director at City of Faith, had become a trusted friend. A tall, black gentleman with a kind face accented by a little salt-and-pepper mustache and close-cut hair, Ricky was as compassionate as anyone I'd ever met. He held me accountable for my actions, and whenever he taught me a life lesson, it was always done in love.

Darren and I set up a time to go meet Ricky at his office at City of Faith, and we were ushered in and sat down across from Ricky's desk on a couple of lounge chairs. It wasn't the first time Darren and Ricky had met. They had spoken once before when McDonald's wanted me to be allowed to attend their Hamburger University program, but there was no way the Louisiana Department of Corrections was going to let me go out of state to Chicago, Illinois for the training.

Darren stated his request. "Well, where are you wanting him to go?" Ricky asked.

"Ruston."

"Ruston? How is he going to get there every day?"

Darren smiled. "We are willing to provide Doug with a vehicle to transport himself back and forth." All three of us knew that's not something most employers would do, even one as awesome as McDonald's.

Ricky looked at me. "How much time have you got left?"

I told him there were about 29 months remaining in my prison sentence.

"We are just going to plead the blood of Jesus over you. Be careful."

That was it. We agreed I could ride my bike to and from the vehicle McDonald's provided. I was being allowed travel freedoms prisoners weren't supposed to have, so we had to do everything we could to keep it under wraps.

The current manager of the Ruston location was a woman who had been there about 25 years but was having to retire due to some health issues. I spent the first month in Ruston training under her. I got there early, stayed late, and worked as many hours as they needed. Recalling the great advice I'd received from Jerrald, I also dedicated that month to being the best team player I could be, not trying to run things in any way until the transition into leadership was completed.

Finally, I started a Bible study with whoever wanted to participate. Most of the staff were typical of the average worker at a McDonald's in Louisiana: young, black males or females anywhere from 18 to 30 years of age. They were a hard-working group, and to my knowledge, they'd never had a white manager before. If they had, it probably wasn't someone who took a genuine interest in who they were.

I wanted to be different than that, someone they could trust as well as respect.

Within four months of first going to work for McDonald's, I had my own store—and in no time our team was meeting all of the company's goals. I also began receiving leadership mentoring from Jennifer, the supervisor of the Ruston store. Even more, I really liked what I was doing, and I felt loyal to McDonald's for giving me the opportunity.

As I focused much of my time on work, I didn't miss church, and I still saw John at some point every day since we shared a room with four other guys. John and I hung out together on the weekends after work or on Sunday between church services. It was becoming obvious, though, that John's relationships with others at church were deepening. At one point, he said to me, "Man, I love you, but you've got to kind of quit riding my coattails. There are people here in my life who are blessing me."

That hurt my feelings a bit. John was my best friend; really, my only friend. I couldn't believe he would tell me something like that, and while I knew he said it in a loving way, I still didn't like hearing it.

Yet it became another defining moment in my life where I realized it was time for me to carve my own way. The two of us had always been going in the same direction, but in different vehicles. John was going to serve the Lord in the church. I was going to serve God in the business world. So, I made it a point to find stuff to do on my own. I became more independent from that day forward.

Back at work, one thing I'd observed about our customers by then is that every McDonald's has a "coffee club," usually an older group of men, business owners in the community, who would come in, enjoy some java, and gab. I figured it was the senior discount on coffee that drew them in. One guy, Clint, would give me the hardest time. I'd bend over backwards to take care of him and the guys, but it never seemed to be enough. He was verbally harsh, short, a bit abrasive, and kind of arrogant. I thought he was a jerk, and at times, I'd have sworn he couldn't stand me.

Imagine my shock, then, when I later found out it was Clint who gave a glowing professional recommendation of me to another businessman in the area—someone who was going to change my life in such a way that I'd forever call him Mister Prince Charming.

~~~~

Danny Prince was an entrepreneur who had several business ventures going in northern Louisiana and Texas, and he was always on the lookout for people he could trust with those ventures. Apparently, Clint had said to Danny one day after coffee club, "You need to come check out this guy over here and see what he has done to McDonald's. It's not even like a McDonald's anymore." McDonald's had gained a reputation for long lines, slow service, and messed up orders, but we didn't have any of that happening at my store.

So, without my knowledge, Danny started coming into the dining room or through the drive-thru to experience it for himself, and he must've liked what he saw. The first time I spoke to Danny was on a Saturday. He was in the dining room, so I went out to clean the lobby and have a meet and greet with him. I was curious and thought I could scout him out a little.

We ended up having a 30-minute conversation. I learned that his office was just down the street, and I became aware he was opening a Burger King inside a travel center/truck stop called Gap Farms along Interstate 20 west of Ruston in Arcadia, Louisiana.

As Danny got up to leave, it became clear he was scouting me out as well.

"Here's my card," he said, handing it to me. "I have some businesses in West Monroe. If you're ever interested in finding out more, just let me know."

I put the card in my wallet. To this day, it's still there.

I returned to the back of the store. *If he's trying to lure me away from McDonald's,* I thought, *there's no way I am going to do that. They gave me a chance when no one else would.* I was proud of my job at McDonald's. At the same time, though, I couldn't help but feel good about his special interest in me.

Looking back at it now, I was often overcompensating, trying to prove that I was not an ex-con. For him to do that made me feel like I could start moving on from that prisoner mentality.

Over the next day or two, whenever my employees asked about Danny, I just told them, "He's just trying to scout us out and see how we do things." I didn't want them to feel threatened or to think in any way that I was going anywhere anytime soon.

Later that week, I agreed to meet with Danny to see those businesses in West Monroe. They were in an upscale shopping strip on Bell Lane with nice brick and stone pillars and arches. It had eight different suites, one vacant, and Danny owned six of them. There was a pharmacy, spa, health food store, and a sandwich and yogurt shop called Counter Culture.

When he asked for my thoughts about the vacant suite, I told him about what I had done previously with Tiger Tan, and he thought a tanning salon might be a good idea for that spot.

I didn't tell Danny that my work at Tiger Tan came prior to a seven-plus year stint in prison.

Then, about a week after that, Danny took me on a ride to Gap Farms. He gave me a tour of the center, introduced me around to the workers, and shared more about his professional history. It was almost as if he were trying to sell himself and his ventures to me, not the other way around. On the way back, Danny took me north of Arcadia to Lake Claiborne to show me his lake home. It was being renovated and was located on a beautiful spot on a tree-covered hill overlooking the water.

The whole trip was incredible. Who doesn't want to feel wanted, and who wouldn't hope that someone would come and sweep them off their feet? We all desire to be and feel significant and to know our worth and value is seen by others. Everyone wants a Prince or Princess Charming to come into their lives.

Danny Prince was quickly becoming that to me.

Three days later, I agreed to meet Danny at his office after work. His was one of many in the suite on Trenton Street, and it was top-end, but not super fancy—kind of like Danny. He ushered me into the office, framed with windows on both the front and sides, and he took a seat across from me instead of behind his desk.

It was then Danny formally asked me to go to work for him.

Instantly, I was nervous, but not about the prospect of becoming Danny's employee. He'd certainly alluded to it enough the past few weeks, so his offer wasn't a surprise.

It was what I had to tell him next that put me on edge.

From my previous experiences revealing my past to a potential employer, I knew I had a 50-50 shot. There were no guarantees, but I also knew that being transparent and honest was a risk I had to take, even if it meant being rejected.

"Before I answer, let me tell you my story."

I told him everything—the drinking, the drugs, my time in prison—all in its nasty glory. He listened intently, his face expressionless the entire time. But I kept going, concluding with where I was presently housed at City of Faith.

"I am actually still serving out my sentence. So, before you hire me, I thought you needed to know all of these things. I am not the man I was. The good Lord got hold of my heart, and I've never been the same since."

All Danny said was, "Honesty is all I ask, and I can definitely work with everything you just told me."

He really was Mister Prince Charming.

~~~~~

I didn't give Danny an answer right away. In fact, for the next two weeks, I struggled with the decision. I'd go to the gym, get on the treadmill, run, and pray obsessively. Just like I had before giving John the go-ahead to get me to City of Faith from my offshore job, I again wanted God to give me a sign. I thought of the story of Gideon from the book of Judges, and of how the Lord placed dew on the wool fleece Gideon had placed on the threshing floor to show him that he was going to lead the Israelites to victory.

"Give me some dew," I prayed. "Anything. Just show me what I need to do."

I hadn't told anyone at McDonald's I was even thinking about another job, much less been offered one. I was secure at McDonald's. I was confident I had a future there. I was content, but I wasn't satisfied in my heart. I knew there was more.

It was scary. Change often is.

But the answer was there the whole time. God had already provided a way for me to continue to advance, just like He'd done every single time before. I just had to seek peace, trust Him, and move forward in faith.

I decided to tell the supervisors at McDonald's what was going on. I started by meeting with Jennifer, who by then had been actively working to elevate me at McDonald's to likely manage several stores at once. She'd made such an investment in me and my career.

I told her I was putting in my notice because I had an opportunity to do something else.

Her face winced with sadness, and she bent forward and stared.

"You can't go," Jennifer said. "We don't get people like you."

My news obviously caught her off guard, and I so appreciated her heartfelt response. It was incredible to be validated by people in authority like her. "I want you to talk to Tony," she directed me, referring to the owner of all the McDonald's stores I'd worked for, and I told her I would.

The next afternoon, as I was on my way to Tony's office, I couldn't help but wonder if perhaps they were going to offer me more money to entice me to stay—and, if they did, how I would respond. I was still kind of torn. I was giving up what I knew and what I had become comfortable with, but I was doing that because I knew there was more out there for me.

Even now, I still feel that way. I don't believe I'm at the pinnacle. God always has more. It's a nice feeling to have.

I arrived, and Tony and I started with an informal conversation about me and my time with McDonald's, which prompted me to ask, "Man, why is it that everybody wants me to stay?"

Tony answered my question with another one. "Do you watch basketball?"

That was the last thing I expected to hear. "Yeah, a little bit," I replied.

"You like the Lakers?"

"That's got to be the most popular team," I said.

"You know who Kobe Bryant is?"

Sure I did. Most non-basketball fans knew Kobe. He was one of the greatest athletes to ever play the game.

"You're like a Kobe Bryant," Tony continued. "Maybe one out of a thousand is like him, and we don't get guys like you very often. When you get a Kobe, you want to keep him on your team."

I leaned back in my chair. *Wow, this dude just compared me to Kobe Bryant*, I thought. *But he still didn't convince me to stay.* As I left to head back to work, my decision was made. Shortly after my arrival, Jennifer called.

"How did it go?" she asked, and I told her what Tony had said about me and Kobe.

I could imagine her shaking her head.

"I'm so mad at Tony," Jennifer said. "I really wanted him to try to pay you to stay. But you know what he told me?

He said, 'Yeah, I could have offered him more money and gotten him to stay, but guys like that aren't made to stay at McDonald's forever. There is more in him. He needs to go on to the next thing.'"

So, I did. The next two weeks, I gave McDonald's everything I had. I worked as much as I could, and there were young men and women there in whom I'd made an investment, training them, teaching them, and making them accountable to do their jobs well. For some of them, nobody had ever given them an opportunity to succeed until me, so it was hard. A lot of people were sad I was leaving, but I did encourage Jennifer to promote my existing assistant manager to take over for me. She did just that, ensuring a smooth transition.

It was time for my next thing.

~~~~

I began working for Danny Prince in April 2010, and right away I got a sense of his style: he'd give me an assignment and set me loose. That was it. No training. No prep. Here's the job. Here's the keys. Just get it done.

One of the first things he had me do was work to implement the membership program I'd used to grow Tiger Tan by applying it to the first class, million-dollar spa that was the cornerstone of the businesses in that shopping strip. The person running the spa was an expert at massage, but he was bad at business. He was territorial with me from the start. I don't know if he felt intimidated, threatened, or both, but I ultimately had to tell him, "Listen. I am just trying to do my job. If you don't like it, you just need to go talk to Danny. But this is what we're doing." That guy was a thorn in my side those first couple of months.

I also provided general oversight, at first, for the health food store located inside the pharmacy, the yogurt shop, and Counter Culture, the sandwich restaurant. In no time, though, I was general manager of all of the businesses, handling everything from hiring and ordering to marketing, advertising, and managing the finances. I'd tell Danny about the mismanagement problems I'd found, but whenever he asked me if he should talk to anyone about them, I took the responsibility.

We were both figuring things out as we went, but I wanted to do whatever it took to make things better, and Danny trusted me to do so.

That was the thing. Being trusted like that was something I was still getting used to. I mean, I'd been given the same trust, to a certain extent, at the company where I worked prior to Tiger Tan, and I'd certainly been trusted at McDonald's. But I found myself still tending to overcompensate for my old prison mentality of not feeling wanted. Behind bars, it largely didn't matter what you did or how good a person you were. The majority of the people that ran the prison system didn't trust me or any of the other inmates. They didn't believe me. This is where it all comes back to what voices we listen to. If we reinforce limiting beliefs about ourselves, they will hold us down and produce thoughts and feelings of inadequacy.

When recidivism rates are taken into account, I suppose their lack of trust was understandable, maybe even justified. So, even though no one I was working with at Danny's businesses knew I was an ex-con, I was surprised to find I still carried that stigma with me and felt I had to offset that distorted view of myself, despite everything that was happening to the contrary.

I pressed forward, and I enjoyed moving around from business to business each day, actively working during busy hours in places like Counter Culture, and meeting so many different people, both staff and customers.

In June, one customer in particular really started catching my eye.

No, she captivated my attention.

She visited Counter Culture pretty much every day for lunch, and she always came to the drive-thru and ordered the same thing: a half-sandwich called the Avocado Delight (our signature sandwich of turkey, mayonnaise, shredded cheddar cheese, and avocados on wheat bread) and a small cup of blueberry yogurt. She was pretty, but she also had a smile—this big, beautiful smile, the friendliest I'd ever seen—that made me think, *Man, her smile is so awesome, it would stop the Rapture!* Kindness just exuded from her.

Thing was, she drove this big, black Tahoe with tinted windows, and she used a different credit card each day to pay for her order. It made me wonder what was going on. *Is she with the Mafia? Or dealing dope? Maybe she's with the FBI?* The multiple card use gave me a perfect excuse to ask the girls working the drive-thru to get her name—which they did, and apparently told me on three different occasions, though I'd get confused because she used so many different cards.

Finally, she told the girls, "You tell him my name is Kristin—and if he can't remember that, then something is wrong with him."

Thankfully, she said that, too, with a smile.

It turned out Kristin was neither an agent of the federal government or a member of a criminal syndicate. She was simply using cards from her parents or her co-workers.

Sufficiently smitten, I began asking the girls to let me know when she was coming up to the drive-thru window so I could go over, hand out her order, and talk with her for a few minutes.

They were the best minutes of my day.

I was never inappropriate. I was never flirtatious. In fact, I thought the ring on her finger meant Kristin was married. With a smile like that, how could she not have a husband, and a happy one at that?

Finally, I got up the courage to find out. As I handed over yet another half-sandwich Avocado Delight and blueberry yogurt, I ventured, "So, I've never seen you come through here with your husband.

"Oh, I'm not married."

"Well, your boyfriend, then."

"I don't have a boyfriend," she replied.

"But you have a ring on your finger," I offered.

"Yes," she said, "but it's not a wedding or engagement ring. It's a gift from my father."

That very instant, I clapped my hands and did a little pirouette, right there at the drive-thru window register.

"Hallelujah!" I shouted. "Man, it is over for you."

I literally did that and said that.

It was so out of character for me. But I couldn't help it.

From that moment on, I just knew Kristin was going to be my wife.

Only problem was, she didn't know it yet.

She also didn't know about my past.

~~~~

A lot happened in the week that followed. One Friday afternoon at work, I was at the front counter of Counter Culture looking out the window and across the parking lot to the entrance of the spa when I saw Kristin leaving the spa. As she walked toward her Tahoe, I went outside and called out, "Hey! What are you doing?"

She turned and smiled, just as I'd anticipated she would.

"I'm about to go to the drive-thru to get me a salad."

"Oh, not tonight you aren't," I said.

She looked befuddled. "Yes, I am. I'm going to get my salad."

"No, you're not."

"Yes, I am."

"No, tonight you're gonna come inside. I'll make you one, and we'll sit down together while you eat it."

It's hard to describe how she looked. She probably couldn't believe my audacity, but she wasn't put off by it, either. With some reluctance and, I hoped, curiosity, she did an about face and headed in my direction.

I didn't pirouette, but I sure wanted to.

I opened the door for her, Kristin went inside, and I followed her and got her order. She took a seat in a red vinyl-covered chair at one of the marbled tables, and I went back behind the counter to prepare her salad. I brought it out to her with some water, her usual beverage choice.

I sat down in the chair across from her. Business was slow that time of day, so we pretty much had the place to ourselves. Not that it mattered. Had it been busy, I still would've given Kristin my full attention. My staff could've handled the rest.

We started talking, and right away, it was almost as if Kristin was laying it all out there. She started by telling me how she doesn't really go out and party.

"I don't either," I replied.

"Well, I don't drink, and I don't go to bars."

"I don't either," I repeated.

She took a bite of her salad and quickly glanced behind me at the big, colorful mural of the name of the business and a big cup of yogurt smothered in fruit toppings at the far end of the dining area.

She then said, "I don't date guys that 'raise the freak flag.'" When I told her I had no idea what that meant, she clarified that the freak flag was waved by men who put off the wrong signals, whether they were weird, creepy, or sexual. "And I don't have sex before I'm married."

Man, it's almost like she's interviewing me, trying to find a way to eliminate me right from the start.

"I don't either," I said again, then added, "You're not the only one that is trying to do the right thing and live the right kind of life."

Kristin seemed to consider that as she took a sip of her water.

"What do you think about kids?" she said.

Whoa, I thought. *That escalated quickly.* Knowing my as-yet-unrevealed past, I carefully considered my reply.

"Well, until today, I haven't met the person with whom I wanted to have any children."

From then on, Kristin opened up about the previous couple of years in her life. For 22 months, her father, Mike, had been valiantly battling two types of lung cancer. She had pretty much put her life on hold to care for her father, help her mom, Judy, and assist with the family's business.

That's also when we talked about me riding past that business on my bike, and I first learned of the nickname her dad had given me: the Blonde Bomber.

As she left to go home, I walked out with her to her vehicle. We got in and I sat down in the passenger seat next to her. Within minutes, her phone rang. The call was brief.

"That was my mom," she said, concern etched on her face. "My dad isn't feeling very good from the latest chemo. I need to go."

"May I pray for you and your father before you leave?"

Kristin agreed, we bowed our heads, and I prayed a simple but heartfelt request that God would take care of her and her family. When I was done, she thanked me, gave me that incredible smile, even if it was noticeably strained, and left.

As I walked back toward the restaurant, I was torn. I felt excited about how our conversation had gone, but how could I celebrate when she was leaving to go home and take care of her dad who was suffering? That call cut right into the moment.

I stayed in touch with Kristin, but that weekend, my mind was all over the place. I also thought about what was happening in the context of who I was. *I am really still in prison, and here I am leading this secret agent lifestyle because I haven't told her yet.*

At that point, I knew I needed to ask Kristin out on a proper date and tell her everything. I talked to a couple of people to get their opinions. First, I called my father and told him all about Kristin and my plan.

"You know, that might not need to be the first thing that you do," he advised.

"No, I think it needs to be," I insisted. "If I really like this person, I'd want them to know right off the bat before we get into this." I said there was something very special about Kristin—about the type of person she was—and I didn't want to mess it up. "Being honest is the key."

Drawing upon his psychology expertise, my father finally relented.

"Well, if you're going to do it, you just need to tell her you're not crazy."

I also talked to Miss Barbara, who by then had been coming in to Counter Culture regularly. I knew she loved me like a momma, and her response reflected that. "I don't know, baby. I don't know if you should do that. I think you should wait." I sensed that Barbara was trying to love and protect me, just in case Kristin had the wrong motives.

I got that, but I didn't think it was really a concern. Of course, John knew about Kristin and how I felt about her, but I didn't seek his advice about the date itself.

Come Monday morning, I called Kristin to see how she was doing and to find out if she was coming by the restaurant that day like usual. When she said she was, I went and bought a single red rose. I gave it to her when she came by the drive-thru for her Avocado Delight, blueberry yogurt, and lunches for everyone at her dad's office—and I asked her if she'd go out to dinner with me.

Kristin said yes, and we agreed to work out the details by phone later. We set the date for the very next night.

I chose El Chico, a Tex-Mex chain that, admittedly, wasn't the nicest restaurant in Monroe, but it was a place I'd eaten at since I was a boy. It was also close to Counter Culture, which was important because I asked Kristin if she would pick me up there and drive us to the restaurant. At first, I was going to offer to follow her there in my car, as strange as that would be. That way, I reasoned, if things went bad during my confession, I could just leave, and she could still finish her meal. But we worked it out for her to get me, and she was fine with that. If things did go south, I'd just have to figure it out on the fly.

Going out like that in public was also nerve racking for me because there was always that feeling that someone would recognize me, either from prison or my days before, and maybe point me out or cause a scene. It was a largely irrational fear, sure, but it was still there, so I did everything I could to stifle it as we drove up, went inside, and were seated at a table.

Since it was a Tuesday night, there weren't that many people there. The server brought water and our menus, and as we awaited his return, I jumped in with both feet.

"Look, there's really something I want to tell you, and it's something I think that you should know."

Kristin had already sensed what I was going to do. "Okay. Well, what is it?"

"I've been to prison before. As a matter of fact, I had a 20-year sentence that I had to serve 10 years on. But the Lord got a hold of my heart, and I've really never been the same since." I took a breath. *Keep going.* "Actually, I'm really still in prison. You know those white vans that you see driving around town dropping guys off here and there? Those guys are at a work release called City of Faith, and that's where I live."

Her first response, considering what I had just revealed, was surprising. "But you have a car."

"Yeah, I do have a car. My boss let me purchase that vehicle. He just takes the money out of my salary, but I'm really not supposed to have it."

"So, what did you do, and how did you get there?" she asked.

For the next three hours, I told her my entire life story in all its ugly yet glorious detail. As I did, Kristin listened intently, hanging on every word. Even today, whenever I share my story, there is always a smile on my face, and it's always the biggest when I'm telling the worst parts. It's a joy for me because I know how the story ends—with God and His incredible grace and love.

One time, Kristin commented, in reference to me having been in prison, "You just don't look like it," and I replied, "One of the things I told myself when I went to prison was that I didn't want to come out looking like I'd been in prison." She interjected other comments such as, "I just never would have guessed," or "I never would have imagined this," or "You couldn't have convinced me to believe that. Are you really telling me the truth?"

I get it. Sometimes I still don't believe it myself.

But that doesn't make it any less true.

We never ordered dinner. I talked, and she listened. When I concluded with my arrival at City of Faith, I asked, "What do you think?"

I felt as though I was blindfolded, standing at the edge of the ship's plank, and not knowing if I was about to be shoved into the shark-infested waters below.

Kristin was succinct.

"Well, I could live with that."

I was *so* glad. I wanted her to accept me, just as I was—and she did.

Then she said, "Wow! We've been here three hours. I really need to go and check on my dad."

With that, we left El Chico, and she dropped me off outside Counter Culture.

I watched that big, black Tahoe pull away, and the same assurance I had that day in the Counter Culture drive-thru when I found out Kristin wasn't married returned. I just *knew* she was going to be my wife.

I had finally found in Kristin what I had been looking for, but never found, in my other relationships, my wild life, my addictions—all of it.

It was awesome and super exciting, but I also knew I had to be patient. There was a whole lot still ahead.

I had to finish my time in prison—and there was another big challenge about to hit.

CHAPTER EIGHT

LOVE, MARRIAGE—
AND SECRETS EXPOSED

THAT DATE WITH KRISTIN took place June 29, 2010. The following night was a Wednesday. I went to church, and they were having a big production to celebrate the Fourth of July coming up that weekend. I'm sure it was festive and patriotic, but I don't remember a thing.

All I could think about was Kristin.

Every day for the next five days, I either spoke with her on the phone or saw her when she came by Counter Culture for lunch. Unbeknownst to me, her parents also came by the drive-thru once, apparently just to get a look at me. I waited on them, though they never introduced themselves. Later, Kristin told me her dad reacted to the rose I had given her with his signature sarcastic humor. "I guess he gives everybody roses that come through the drive thru, huh?" she said her father had kidded. "I think I'm gonna go get me a rose."

Well, he didn't get his flower that day, but he did like what he saw.

On July 5, Kristin presented me with an unusual request. "Would you like to go look at some houses with me?"

Man, she must really like me. I thought. *Why else would she ask me to pick out a house with her?* "Yeah, I'll go."

She picked me up that afternoon, and we looked at a couple of homes. Her friend was a real estate agent, and I imagine the houses were nice, though I don't recall much about them, preoccupied as I was.

Is this just her and her new guy friend hanging out? Is she asking me to do this with her because she knows she's going to marry me? It drove me nuts.

But it was a lot of fun.

Whenever I returned to City of Faith each night, I always left my cellphone hidden because I wasn't really supposed to have a phone as it was. Therefore, the first thing I did every morning when I got in the vehicle to go to work was check my voice mail to see if Kristin had called.

It was the morning of July 6, exactly one week after our date at El Chico, that I saw Kristin had called, but not left a message. It was early, but I called back right away.

One of her friends answered.

"Kristin needs you. Her dad just passed away."

I shouldn't have been shocked, knowing the situation, but I still was.

"Where is she? What can I do to help?"

Her friend replied, "I'll have Kristin call you in a little bit."

I found out later that, at that moment, Kristin and her family were waiting on the coroner to arrive to remove the body from the hospital.

I was at work by the time Kristin was able to call me back. "My dad passed away overnight at Saint Francis Medical," she told me. "He got so bad we took him in. Everything happened so fast after that."

I heard the anguish in her voice. "Can I come by? Can I bring anything?"

She simply said to bring myself.

"I'll be there by 11 o'clock," I told her.

I went to the hospital to show my respects and be there for Kristin in whatever way she needed. I kept to the background, but I could hear some people whispering, "Isn't that the guy from Counter Culture? What is he doing here?" Kristin later confirmed that most of them didn't know she had asked me to come, much less that we had gone out on a date.

After that, I showed up at the wake, the funeral, the graveside service, and even the family's house after that service. I met her older brother, Shane, who had spina bifida, was in a wheelchair, and lived with her mom, as well as her sister, Kelly—but my only motivation was to be there to support Kristin. She and I spoke briefly during those awful days, and I attempted to keep any conversation light. I knew she was hurting, and I could relate somewhat after my experience with my mom's death. But no loss of a parent is ever the same. Each one is unique and carries its own devastation for the child.

In the weeks after her father's burial, along with still picking up lunches for her and everybody else at the office, Kristin came to Counter Culture after work just about every day and stayed until we closed at nine o'clock. Quickly, but quite naturally, we grew closer.

Being with Kristin was so different from any other relationship I'd previously had with a woman. Before, regardless of what I may have believed back then, it was always about hooking up and partying. But with Kristin, it wasn't about any of that. It wasn't sexual, even though I was strongly attracted to her. It was pure. I wasn't trying to sleep with her, and she didn't want anything from me. We sat in the office for hours talking. We didn't discuss anything terribly serious. We just talked, and I enjoyed our conversations. Even more, I enjoyed her presence.

We were becoming friends—and, in the process, more than friends.

One day in late July, I had to run over to Ruston to drop off some paperwork at the corporate headquarters and meet with Danny. I knew Kristin and her family were getting ready to leave in a few days for a week-long getaway to Alabama's Gulf Coast, and I had been thinking about telling her something for days.

I called Kristin while I was driving. I didn't really know if I was going to say anything when she answered, but it was something that had been welling up within me, and I just couldn't keep it in any longer.

"Look, I need to tell you something."

She paused. "Well, what is it?"

"I'm in love with you."

I quickly added, "Now, don't say anything, because I didn't say that for you to say something back."

As requested, Kristin didn't reply right then—but a couple of days later, we did talk about my declaration, and we discussed our feelings for one another. We did this on the phone, which was probably easier for her. I know it was for me. That's probably why I used a call to tell her I was in love with her in the first place.

"You know," Kristin began, "I have just been thinking about what you said."

"Look, I didn't say that to get a response from you," I repeated. "I just had it in me and needed to let you know what I was feeling."

"I know—but I think I'm in love with you, too."

My heart raced with a surge of joy.

"I'm going to marry you after I get out of prison," I declared. "Will you wait for me?"

It wasn't a proper proposal, but again, I had it in me, and it had to come out.

She didn't say "yes" right then, but she didn't say "no," either, and I never pressed Kristin to give me an answer. I just wanted her to know what my intentions were.

Three days into her family vacation, Kristin called me. I was at the gym on a cardio machine.

"You know," she said, "I was talking to my friends and asking them what they thought about having a wedding on the beach. They were kind of discouraging me from doing that—about getting married to you. But I thought about it, and I want to do it. What do you think? Want to get married on the beach?"

I stopped the cardio device. If it's possible to *hear* someone smile, I heard Kristin's sweet smile that very moment on the phone.

"Man, that is awesome. I'm all in!" I told her. "I can't wait until I get out of prison."

It was probably small talk after that, for all I remember. I was just so happy. I felt like I'd just won the lottery.

Kristin wants to marry me!

Then I thought, *Now all I have to figure out is how to get a ring—and give her a proper proposal.*

~~~~

I had very limited access to money, in that anything I earned was put into an account that was managed by City of Faith. I was allowed to spend some, but not all, of the funds. That's understandable, since the whole idea was for me to have a good amount of money to work with once my prison time ended. But I was determined to get Kristin a ring, and I told her as much.

"I really want to get you a ring," I insisted one evening during one of our visits at Counter Culture.

"You can get me a ring when you get out of prison," she replied kindly.

"No," I told her. "I can't *not* get you a ring." My spoken grammar was lousy, but it got the point across.

"It's okay. I really don't have to have a special ring right now. We'll pick out something together when you are released."

But I was stubborn as a mule and would not be deterred. I ended up scraping together $1,200 from funds I had diligently saved from monthly incentive bonuses from my McDonald's days and my portion of the tip money from Counter Culture.

I went to Flair Fine Jewelers in Monroe and bought Kristin a diamond band.

Well, it wasn't diamonds, per se. More like diamond flakes.

But it was what I could afford, and it sure sparkled.

Ring in hand, it was time to figure out the proposal. I called Kristin's mom. We called her Doo Dee, a nickname her husband had given her. I suppose it rhymed with Judy.

"I want to surprise Kristin and ask her to marry me. Are you okay with that?"

By then, Doo Dee really liked me and had no reservations about my desire to marry her daughter. She responded as she often did, dripping with lovely southern charm and grace.

"Well, yes, that sounds good," she drawled.

"I want it to be a surprise," I added. "Can we plan to have dinner at your house one night? I'll come over and cook or whatever."

Admittedly, my plan wasn't terribly well thought out, but Doo Dee seemed happy enough. "That'd be nice," she replied, and we set things in motion for the upcoming Friday.

It was just Kristin, Doo Dee, and her older brother, Shane. I made oven fried chicken. I'd cooked a few times for Kristin and her family before, starting with steak. The first time I had prepared oven fried chicken, the oven temperature wasn't quite right for some reason, and I thought the food was dry and overdone. No one complained, but the requests for extra ketchup spoke for themselves. I saw this as my chance at redemption on the dish—and everyone seemed to like it. Good thing, too, since Kristin had already kidded more than once, "Yeah, whoever I marry is going to have to love to cook." I'd always say, "Well, *I* love to cook!" in hopes she'd take the hint. Before I met her, I really hadn't cooked anything since I got out of prison. I guess I was still pretty good in the kitchen.

Meal finished, we were all sitting at the dining room table, with me at the head where her father had undoubtedly sat before he got sick, when I made my move.

"Man, I forgot my gum out in the car," I blurted while standing up. "Does anybody want some?"

No, it wasn't a brilliant excuse to leave, but it was all I could come up with. When I returned inside, I reached in my pocket for the gum—and instead pulled out the box with the ring. I opened it as I got down on one knee in front of Kristin.

I imagine Doo Dee was smiling, and I heard Shane, a sensitive little rascal, start to cry, but I only had eyes for Kristin. She was positively beaming with that uncontainable smile of hers.

"I've been waiting for a woman like you my whole life. I want to know if you'll spend the rest of your life with me. Will you marry me?"

It was such an emotional moment. There I was, proposing to Kristin at her family's home, and her dad wasn't there to witness it. He wouldn't be there to give her away at the wedding. It had only been weeks since he'd passed away. It was bittersweet. Poignant.

Yet Kristin's answer set the sadness aside.

"Yes."

~~~~~

That was August 20—but we couldn't rightfully set a date for the wedding yet because I had to confirm exactly when I was being released from prison. I knew my 10 years weren't due to be up until early April 2011, but I went online to the State of Louisiana website, hoping against hope that maybe something had changed in the laws so I could secure my release a little earlier.

Incredibly, I stumbled across a bill, Act 649, that had been signed by Governor Bobby Jindal. I read in amazement as I learned that the law, when it went into effect October 15, retroactively changed the calculation on the reduction of my sentence for good behavior. I was supposed to get 30 days for every 30 days served, but the formula had increased to 35 days "good time" for every 30 incarcerated.

I quickly did the math in my head. I was no engineer, but it seemed to add up that I could be released the day the law went into effect: October 15.

Though it was still early in the morning, I contacted Paul, who worked in the administration office at City of Faith, and he confirmed that, yes, they were recalculating my sentence, and yes, October 15 was going to be my last day in prison.

The 20-year sentence had indeed become 10 years—and a bit less.

Then I called Kristin. I woke her up.

"Oh, you won't believe this!" I said, unable to hide my excitement. "Would you still marry me if something changed with my sentence?"

"Yeah," she said. "What do you mean?"

"I mean, would you marry me sooner?"

"What are you talking about?"

I told her—and we just laughed with joy.

Within four months of us meeting, and five days after a miracle that released me early from prison, Kristin and I got married. Most people couldn't believe it, and many others didn't think it would last. Even more weren't sure about our motives. *Who* is this guy, just out of prison, that swooped in after her dad died and has taken advantage of this poor girl?

All I knew is I'd waited and prayed a long time for a wife, and she was the one.

We set the wedding date for October 20. On October 15, I checked out of City of Faith, and Kristin had agreed to let me stay with her at her house until we were married. I bunked in her spare bedroom. My brother, Mark, who had been in and out of jail three times during my prison sentence, was also released the same day I was. Kristin lovingly agreed to let him stay with us, too, just for a short time until I could help him get settled and find his own place. Mark camped out on the living room couch. On top of all that, I had to take care of some final things with my parole officer, and I needed to make sure everything kept running smoothly with the businesses Danny had entrusted to me.

It just seemed like there wasn't enough time to do anything, but Kristin and I were determined not to delay the marriage.

Therefore, those five days between my release and our wedding were busy and, at times, trying. So, by the time we began our drive down to Gulf Shores, Alabama for the event itself, we were both nervous and a bit on edge. In all of the rush, we had neglected getting a marriage license, so we had to stop somewhere in Alabama along the way to get one. I kept getting turned around and sidetracked trying to find the correct courthouse in Baldwin County, knowing we had to get to the Palm Beach Resort in Gulf Shores in time for the ceremony. Kristin had already set up everything, and our families had gone there ahead of time to wait on us.

But it's kind of hard to have a wedding without a bride and groom.

Flustered and frustrated, we finally got the license in Fairhope, a little town across the bay from Mobile, Alabama, but Kristin desperately wanted to stop to get her nails done and feared there wouldn't be enough time to do so. "Listen," I said, "it is you and I getting married. They are not going to start this wedding without us, so we're going to stop and find a place for you to get your nails done."

We found a perfect little salon in Foley, Alabama, just a few miles north of Gulf Shores, and as Kristin got the manicure, it seemed to calm her. I settled down as well while I walked around inside a Winn-Dixie grocery store next door— so when we did get to the hotel, Kristin and I were still on time and our shared jitters had worn off.

The hotel was something out of a dream, and the simple setting and decorations on the beach were beautiful. Kristin had found a photographer who also doubled as a pastor to perform the wedding, and in attendance on my side of the tiki torch-lined aisle were my dad, stepmom, and brother. Representing Kristin were her mom and two siblings. The whole thing cost a few hundred dollars, but we didn't care. It was perfect, an intimate, family wedding.

I wore white linen pants and a pale green linen shirt accented by a boutonniere of white lime roses and dark purple calla lilies to match her corsage and bridal bouquet. I was super high with anticipation as I stood next to the pastor close to the beach, Mark at my side. But when I saw Kristin, dressed elegantly in a strapless white gown, coming down the aisle escorted by my father, everything within me went instantly at peace.

She was stunning.

We didn't prepare anything special, no self-styled vows or music. It was a basic ceremony with all of eight people in attendance, but we had a backdrop that was anything but ordinary. It was near sunset, the lavender sky merging with the gulf waters beyond. God outdid Himself for us.

Looking back at that wonderful day, I just knew it was the Lord's doing. Everything that had happened in my life up to that point—good, bad, and in-between—was orchestrated by Him. Sometimes crazy and never boring, no one could convince me that it wasn't God's handiwork. Only He could take a life as messed up as mine and turn it into the masterpiece it was going to become with Kristin at my side.

The words that I'd first said to myself back in 2004 when I heard Pastor David Otis' guest speaker talk about his early prison release resonated once more.

"Why not me!"

Before we got married, Kristin and I didn't talk very much about our past relationships. On my end, I didn't see the point. Kristin was first class. There was no comparison between her and any of the other women I'd been with. For me, the past was in the past, and that's where it needed to stay.

For her part, Kristin had told me she'd been married once before, but she didn't share anything more than that, and that was fine with me, too.

Without fully knowing why, Kristin and I both felt like our marriage was truly a fresh, new start.

We each had been given a clean slate.

But there was still some stubborn chalk dust, ghostly shadows of the past, that needed to be fully erased.

~~~~

October 20 was a Wednesday, and our honeymoon at the resort lasted into the weekend. We returned to Monroe on Sunday, and we settled in that night, as all newlyweds do, not really knowing what to expect next.

Every fear that Kristin had from every one of her past relationships—fears I knew nothing about—started creeping out right away. They manifested through her insecurity as she questioned me daily about where I'd been and who I was talking to, things she had never asked about before we got married. It didn't help that I was not someone who just automatically opened up about stuff like that. I wasn't a good communicator in a way that would help grow her trust in me. As a result, I felt like she was interrogating me, and I easily became defensive.

Kristin also constantly called me out in public, thinking I was looking at other women when that wasn't at all what I was doing. When I was an inmate, and even when I was in the work release at City of Faith, I didn't look around much at the world. It was an almost paranoid prisoner mentality that instinctively told me to keep a low profile and make sure no one was out to get me.

Once I was free, that wasn't an issue anymore. I wanted to look at everything, and as Kristin misread that, I felt like I unjustifiably had to defend my character. When I was in prison, I'd read Christian books about marriage, and I knew all about "bouncing my eyes" in public (a term to describe a man seeing a pretty woman and looking away before he began to desire her, with its biblical origin from the "covenant" Job made with his eyes in Job 31:1). But I hated having to argue my case with the woman who I thought hung the moon.

Still, I did, time and again, and it led to quite a few spats between us.

Finally, Kristin's life, which had already had its share of abrupt change with the death of her father followed by our marriage, was being further disrupted. She had lived alone for a couple of years. Not only was I now living with her, but so was Mark. That speedily became a flash point because she saw far better than I did how co-dependent my brother and I were with one another. In no time, she gave me an ultimatum. "Look, I love your brother, but he has to find a place to live. This can't go on."

She was right, and I quickly helped Mark move on after that—but the seeds of discontent had been sown, watered, and were growing like weeds in our young relationship.

At the same time, we decided we wanted to have children. That was a big deal, in that as a young teenager, Kristin had been diagnosed with endometriosis. It's often a painful disorder where tissue similar to that which normally lines the inside of the uterus grows outside the uterus. Because of it, she was told by a doctor that she would never be able to have a baby. She had lived with that dire prognosis her entire life.

Nevertheless, we wanted to try—and not long after we were married, she became pregnant. Though I know she was scared, Kristin was excited. I was, too, though it was everything I could do to set aside my own fear about being a father after how miserably I had failed at it years earlier before going to prison.

Nine weeks into the pregnancy, Kristin began to experience pain and bleeding. We went to the doctor—only to discover that Kristin's regular doctor, who she'd had since she was a teenager, was out of town. We met instead with a doctor she had never seen before, and he had a horrible bedside manner. My wife was hurting and frightened, but he just looked at her and said, "Yep, you're losing the baby." He did add, "This happens sometimes," I guess to try to be reassuring, but he was very matter-of-fact about it all. It was awful.

Kristin believed he was in a rush because he had to leave to deliver a baby, but that was hardly an excuse. Even worse, he didn't give her any advice or anything for the pain. It was just, "Go home and wait for your doctor to come back."

Luckily, Barbara and Kevin were there for us. We didn't know what to do or what to expect, and it was going to be several days before we could go back in to see Kristin's regular doctor.

It was during this time that Kristin had a powerful encounter with the Holy Spirit. She was sitting on our couch in the living room, and God spoke to her, saying, "Worship me, O barren woman." In her surprise and sorrow, Kristin laughed and responded, "I'm not worshipping you, and I am not barren."

She heard His voice say it again, then a third time. "Okay, fine," she conceded. She then picked up her phone, used it to turn on some worship music, and began to weep. Kristin said it was followed by a tangible presence that felt like a hug. She described it as a steadiness that she'd never felt before in her entire life.

She remained in that place of weeping and worshipping until, a couple of days after the visit to the doctor, I was at work at Counter Culture and Kristin called from home.

"I think I passed the baby."

I went home as quickly as I could. What had come out of her was small, about half the size of a pill bottle. Right there in the bathroom, she told me for the very first time the story about what the Lord had told her.

As worship music played in the background, we decided that we were not going to flush it down the toilet. Instead,

I said we needed to have a little burial. We found a bottle, put the tissue inside, and dug a hole next to our home. We held each other and cried in disbelief.

That moment took us in a different direction as a couple in our relationship with God. It was the beginning of really learning how to be intimate and vulnerable with the Lord through worship.

After that, Kristin would be on the living room couch as I left for work each morning, and when I came home each afternoon, Kristin would still be there. In her despair, she'd hardly moved. After a couple of days of this, I told Kristin she was going to have to pull herself up and out of it. I had to figure out how to be the brave soldier to help her out because she was falling to pieces, but I didn't have any experience to draw from. I tried to be strong and let my emotions release and be evident, but I also wanted to console and comfort Kristin. It was difficult trying to figure out how to be the support that she needed me to be while knowing that I didn't want her to continue in that mode any longer than was necessary.

Four days after what we believed was the full miscarriage, we went in to see her doctor, who had just returned to the hospital. Kristin had an incredibly close relationship with her doctor, and as she shared what had happened during the last appointment, her doctor was not happy at all.

She called the other doctor we'd seen and expressed her unhappiness quite vividly. She then examined my wife, and instantly became more concerned.

"Kristin, I'm so sorry."

"You're so sorry for what?" Kristin asked.

"You've got to get to the hospital, and I've got to do emergency surgery on you. The baby is still in you."

We couldn't believe it. Apparently, Kristin had exceeded the amount of time to have a dead fetus inside of her without her body going into shock and falling into sepsis. We didn't know this. Nobody had told us.

Kristin was operated on that very afternoon in February 2011—and as she came out of the anesthesia, she had another amazing experience. At first, she asked for her father. "Your dad's not here," the doctor said, "but we will get him in a minute. We will go ask your mom where he is."

Kristin asked again before remembering that her father had died. But her request was understandable. While she was under, Kristin recalled seeing her dad standing at the end of the bed. Jesus was with him, as was another woman she didn't recognize. Kristin then saw a full-term baby pulled out of her and handed over to her father.

My wife saw what was actually happening to our baby in heaven.

Kristin recovered from the procedure and was sent home, but she couldn't figure out the identity of the other woman she saw in her divine vision. About a week later, we went to church, and that Sunday morning there was a guest speaker. Incredibly, he spoke about what happens to babies who die, saying that guardian angels are set aside for each child, usually a grandparent or some other loved one who had passed away and was already in heaven. He had no clue we had just lost our baby.

When we got home, Kristin went into my office at home, looking for something in my desk. She opened a drawer and saw a photograph.

"Doug? Who is this woman?"

I smiled. "That's my mom."

Kristin gasped. "She was the one, in the room with my dad when I was operated on! They are watching over our baby in heaven with Jesus."

We immediately texted our pastor, who just happened to be having lunch with that guest speaker. Kristin told them what happened, and we got on the phone with them. All of us cried. To this day, Kristin says it was the Lord who led her to go into my office so she could see that photo—and whenever Kristin and I share that story today, we still feel overwhelmed by the magnitude of what Jesus was, and still is, willing to do to restore us when we're hurting.

~~~

Despite all that God had done to meet us in our pain and hardship before and after the miscarriage, things got worse in our relationship. It seemed to me almost like Kristin was trying to sabotage our marriage and push me away, but I wouldn't have it. "There ain't nothing that you are going to do that is going to make me run away," I told her one day. "I spent all of this time waiting on you, and I promise you, what you are trying to do is not going to get me to run off."

In addition to the baggage I brought along with me from all of my previous and markedly dysfunctional relationships with women, there were some severe issues behind Kristin's behavior. Problem was, she truly didn't know about them yet, so neither did I.

It was bad.

We sought counsel to learn how to better cope with one another by meeting individually with Kevin and Barbara— me with him, and Kristin with her. We weren't very good at it, though. In my times with Kevin, all I did was blame everything on my wife. I wasn't mean about it, just like I wasn't intentionally harsh to her. Yet Kristin would come home and say, "Well, Miss Barbara says" this about a particular issue. "Miss Barbara said you were just never going to be deep."

I'd sarcastically joke, "Man, Miss Barbara says this. Miss Barbara says that. I don't care what Miss Barbara says." I didn't like anyone telling me I *couldn't* do something, but I also knew that was the cry of Kristin's heart, to have somebody with whom she could share her ugly thoughts, feelings, and emotions without judgment.

I tried to be gentle and understanding, but I got easily worn down by it all. I know Kristin did, too. We were both trying to figure out how to deal with each other's issues.

Then, in her conversations with Barbara, Kristin began bringing up some things from her childhood and adolescence that were troubling and too much for Barbara. She told Kristin, "Baby, I love you, but you've got some stuff I can't help you with." She gave Kristin the name and number of somebody who could, a counselor named Diane Phillips.

Right after Kristin started seeing Diane, she told me, "Doug, I know this may sound crazy, but I feel like I've been sexually abused."

She said I just looked at her and played it off cool, but on the inside, I was losing it.

"I think it was by family members," she added, "but I don't have a vivid memory of it. It's a feeling, one of sick repulsion."

As she met with Diane, Kristin began to recall repressed memories of multiple men, family members and friends of family members, who had violated her body. As they came out, her and Diane started working through the trauma the abuse had caused.

Most of all, Diane's counseling changed my wife's life as she revealed to Kristin a Jesus she never knew before. She discovered a Jesus who came to a place in her life that she thought was so dirty, shameful, and nasty that nobody would come there. Yet she said Jesus came, sat in it with her, and showed her where He was. He also revealed to her that, through forgiveness, He would make it as though the abuse had never happened.

Kristin said, "I had never had anybody come to me that way. Ever. I remember locking eyes with Jesus that day, and I haven't taken my eyes off Him since. I've never known a love and compassion and mercy like that. When Diane told me that she was going to invite Jesus into this place and asked if I minded if He came, I felt the safest I ever had in my life, even though I hadn't grown up in church, when she said the name of Jesus. I didn't see angels or hear trumpets, but the peace that filled my body was enough for me. I said, 'Sure, if He wants to come. I don't know if He will.'"

"But He did. He came willingly. It made me realize what a gentleman Jesus was because He wasn't going to overstep and come if I said He couldn't. He came into my hiding place where I hid in shame, and He uncovered it and told me how beautiful I was and how beautiful this would be. I was in such a desperate place, but there was such a powerful, peaceful presence. It was like everything inside of me awakened to my Creator. I couldn't say 'no.' I couldn't say 'no' to the one who had created me, loved me, and who came to set me free. He walked with me through each story of abuse and empowered me to forgive. He captivated my heart through His captivation of me. His adoration for me still takes my breath away."

During that same session, Diane told Kristin, "I want you to show you what Doug looks like to you."

"Jesus put out His hand like He was presenting something to me," Kristin said, "and Doug was there. I'll never forget, it was like he popped out of this gift box for me and was covered in the most beautiful, bright light. I'd never pictured Doug like that. From that moment on, it was like I went on a journey to realize that Doug really is *good*. He really was for me and he was not going to hurt me."

"After we got married, I realized I needed help, but I wasn't sure with what. There were patterns of behavior I didn't like about myself. These patterns were negative and were starting to disrupt my marriage and how I viewed my husband. Doug was paying a price for something he didn't do, and I didn't want to hurt him anymore with my negative behavior toward him," Kristin said. "The Lord healed me with a husband who was never going to hurt me or cheat on me or lie to me or even have one thought about another woman. The redemption was beautiful."

Kristin shared with me everything about the abuse openly and with no reservations, and, of course, one of my first reactions was shock. I couldn't believe that someone could do that to the woman I loved. I had to process it and learn to accept it.

But at the same time, deep inside of me, I was holding on to my own shame and guilt from my past, and I didn't know if I was ever going to be confident or courageous enough to let Kristin know about it the same way she was with me.

Yet even as I struggled with that, Kristin began to change, and so did I. In the mornings, I'd go into the spare bathroom, turn on the light, and sit there and read the Bible. It was an odd place, perhaps, to get away and be alone, but it was there where I'd read God's Word over and over. During those quiet moments, I came to realize that I needed to love Kristin without any restrictions, stipulations, or barriers.

I made a conscious decision that there was only one way that was going to happen—and that was by me putting everything I had into figuring out what I needed to do to be the best husband possible. I had spent my whole life living the wrong way. Everything I could do wrong, I did. It was time for me to start figuring out how to do everything right. I had to mature into the type of husband that Kristin needed me to be, and more importantly, the husband that God created me to be.

In a conversation about that one afternoon with my stepmom, she told me something so very basic yet incredibly wise. "You know, you just have to love your wife the way that Christ loved the church."

I had read that exhortation from the Apostle Paul in Ephesians 5:25 plenty of times before, but it was like I was suddenly hearing it for the very first time. My quest from that point forward was to love Kristin in a practical way that fulfilled that passage—to love her exactly how she needed to be loved, all the time, no matter what she was struggling with and regardless of how I felt or didn't feel. One of the hardest things for me to do was to train myself to simply *listen* to Kristin and not let my mind wander to whatever else was going on at that moment. I wanted her to know that I cared about how she felt and what she thought, but I had to diligently teach myself how to do that in order to truly value my relationship with her.

In our times with Barbara and Kevin, they helped us see the difference between baggage and luggage. Baggage is usually something you just drag along from place to place, but luggage is something that you use when you go on a trip. When we learned to see our past issues in that light, it gave us a different understanding of some of the things that kept creeping back into our relationship, stuff that we should have gotten rid of but were still toting around with us. That realization allowed us to start traveling onward in our journey as a couple.

Before we got married, Kristin and I had said we wanted our marriage to be different than anything else we'd ever seen before. Neither one of us were willing to settle for less than what had been placed in our hearts, and our values stayed lined up even when our emotions or feelings did not. There was always an easier way out if we wanted to take it, but we always went back to that commitment. Saying it and living it out were sometimes two different things, but we were determined—and it was beginning to work.

But could we keep it up?

———

CHAPTER NINE

FINDING YOUR NEW DAY

IT WAS GOING TO BE A BIG LEAP OF FAITH, especially for Kristin, to try to get pregnant again after the miscarriage. She certainly didn't want to go through the loss and pain a second time. Neither did I.

It was April 2012 when some friends, Greg and Abigail, came by Counter Culture. They were from Georgia, and we had met them just after the beginning of the new year when Abigail started bringing her kids to the restaurant after school for a snack. We gradually got to know them and even had them over for dinner, but we weren't really close to them at that point.

They saw us as they were going through the drive-thru and Kristin and I were heading into the store. They called Kristin over to talk, and I headed inside and sat near the main counter while I waited for her. I wasn't on a regular shift, and I'd gone on inside to do payroll.

Abigail asked Kristin how she was doing. "Well, that's funny," Kristin replied. "I just left the grocery store and I saw this baby. For the first time, I realized I didn't want to look at the child. I just had a numb feeling. So, I don't really know how I am doing."

Not only did Greg and Abigail know we had lost our baby, but they had lost three of their own. Abigail asked Kristin, "How long has it been since you had the miscarriage? Have you had your cycle?"

"Yeah," Kristin told her. "I've had two."

"Well," Abigail responded, "you need to go home and make love to your husband."

What? Kristin thought. *Come on, man. Couldn't you just pray for me in Jesus' name or something?* Kristin really didn't know Abigail well enough for her to speak that way into her life, but there it was.

Dumbfounded, Kristin replied, "Why would I do that?" The doctor had given us the okay medically to begin trying, but Kristin was hesitant.

Her friend certainly wasn't. "As you open up your body, you're actually opening your heart to the Lord to receive the gift He is about to give you."

That's when Kristin said she just knew the Lord was all over it.

Kristin hugged Abigail through the car window, came inside, and walked right up to me.

"We need to go home and make love."

I wasn't expecting to hear that, especially given our circumstances, but how else could I respond to such a directive? I excused myself from the staff and Kristin and I left.

Kristin cried the entire time we made love. I asked if she was okay, and she assured me she was fine. She later said, "I was opening myself up, but I was scared as Hades. I had to trust that what I was hoping for was going to come about."

As I said, it was an incredible leap. After all, before she'd gotten pregnant the first time, Kristin had completed a 21-day fast. It was the first time she had ever fasted as a sign of her faith in God, but she did it anyway. Then we lost the baby.

To say the least, it was a stretch when she realized God was asking us to try again and trust Him. Quite honestly, her first thought was, *Yeah, we did, and you see how well that worked out.* But deeper down, from the depths of her soul, she cried out, *Okay, I'm going to believe—and we will trust you, Lord!*

About five weeks later, Kristin heard the Lord direct her to take a pregnancy test. She went to the store and brought five tests, took them, and every one of them were positive.

When I got home from work, Kristin told me she was pregnant once again. "I knew the voice of the Lord," she said later, "so no matter how scary and unstable it felt, I had that peace. It's not like a regular voice. It is the creator God voice that calms every storm."

As the pregnancy progressed, Kristin battled the fear of another miscarriage. Even more, she wondered if there was going to be something wrong with the baby should she carry it to term. Her brother had spina bifida. Both her and her sister had experienced seizures after they were born.

Kristin's concerns were constant and real, but she combated them by consistently crying out to the Lord. She often says desperation is her gift—as is genuine vulnerability. If someone asks her how she's doing, she'll usually tell them. Like she did with Abigail, she won't be insensitive or anything, or go into any great detail, but she's discovered how to be open and honest with others and the Lord.

Kristin says God values our humanity way more than we do. He understood that she was scared. He understood that it was a risk for her. He knew her past. But He absolutely loved that she just kept coming back to Him, finding His presence. She says God told her, "Kristin, your greatest weapon is your great awareness to my presence upon you and around you."

She says she's never forgotten that. She calls it her anchor. As she later put it, "I was scared as heck the whole nine months, but I stayed incredibly open and honest about it. I allowed myself to be human and not pretend like I wasn't struggling. For me, it was when I heard the voice of the Lord. It's Jesus for me. It is the presence of God that lives on the inside of me and is constantly speaking to me and loving me. It is how I center myself."

For my part, Kevin reminded me that Kristin's emotions were going to go up and down. "How did you feel when you were doing drugs?" he asked me.

"Some made me high, some brought me down, and some made me crazy," I said.

"So, when you did cocaine? Xanax? Drank? All at once?"

"Yeah, I was all over the place emotionally," I told him.

Kevin laughed. "That's the way Kristin's going to be when she's pregnant."

So, I did everything I could to minimize anything that was going to rock her boat. As she gained weight from the pregnancy, I thought my wife was the most beautiful thing in the world, but Kristin didn't believe that was how I felt, so we still had to deal with some security issues.

We were also coming to terms with the fact that we were going to be parents. It was about to be the real deal, a whole new level of family, and in many ways, that frightened both of us.

~~~~~

In addition to those personal issues, I found myself in the midst of a huge transition at work. It began with Danny transferring me from Counter Culture and the other businesses I was overseeing in that shopping center to being in charge of the travel center along Interstate 20 at Gap Farms.

I should have seen it as a compliment on my abilities as a manager, but I took it as an insult. I mean, a travel center in Arcadia, Louisiana? Really? It was neither glam nor glorious, and I inherited a mess. Now, I'm not the type of person who doesn't try to fix problems no matter how dissatisfied I am, but I did it with a bad attitude that only got worse as I commuted back and forth every day.

I didn't realize what God was up to. He was giving me opportunities to experience new management roles and tactics that I'd need later on. I just didn't see it that way at first.

But I slowly came around. I remember reading the passage in 1 Timothy 3 where it talks about the qualifications of overseers and deacons in the church. It says the overseer "is to be above reproach, faithful to his wife, temperate, self-controlled, respectable, hospitable, able to teach, not given to drunkenness, not violent but gentle, not quarrelsome, not a lover of money. He must manage his own family well and see that his children obey him, and he must do so in a manner worthy of full respect. (If anyone does not know how to manage his own family, how can he take care of God's church?) He must not be a recent convert, or he may become conceited and fall under the same judgment as the devil. He must also have a good reputation with outsiders, so that he will not fall into disgrace and into the devil's trap." (1 Timothy 3:2-7)

I thought to myself, *Man, I've been missing it.* I came to the conclusion that what I thought about myself was a form of pride. I was always trying to defend myself, to prove myself—and that only went to prove that I hadn't arrived yet. I still had a ways to go as a Christian man. I was an overseer, a shepherd, of Gap Farms, Counter Culture, and most of all, of my own home. With God's help, I knew I needed to do better.

So, four months into what would become a six-month stay at Gap Farms, Danny and I met at his office in Ruston for a special meeting where I rolled up my sleeves—and made amends with him. I shared all the details of what I was learning from Scripture and how I was applying it to myself as a person. I admitted I was being so lousy I probably would have fired myself. I knew God, and I had spent so much time in His Word. I was convicted, and I wanted to improve.

Two things happened when he and I had that conversation. First, I bared my heart and soul to Danny, not caring what he said in response. He knew that, and I think he saw something in me, something *of* me, that he had never seen before.

Second, dating back to 2010, Danny had told me about a property that he someday wanted to turn into a rehabilitation center. He hadn't done much about it since then, but after our meeting, I believe he decided to make it come to pass.

But it still didn't happen instantly. In fact, Danny first moved me back to Counter Culture from Gap Farms for a few more months before he started working in earnest on the rehabilitation center. In the meantime, I changed my attitude about my work. I came against any dissatisfaction that had set in, and I remembered that there wasn't anything I couldn't figure out. I did everything with utmost excellence. I was determined to be the very best overseer of whatever it was I was given to do. I began to see myself succeeding at the rehabilitation center even if I felt I didn't have a clue what I was doing.

I'd drive down the interstate, see that building off in the distance, and begin to plan. To dream. I became pregnant with it.

I knew that's what God was telling me to do next—and I couldn't see myself doing anything else.

That center became what is now New Day Recovery. I didn't come up with the name. That was Danny's idea. He said, "Everybody needs a new day!" But I developed its mission—and pretty much everything else. Its vision reads, "Participants who complete the New Day Recovery program will have a life that is transformed so that they lead a purpose-driven life that is free of drugs and alcohol. Individuals will engage in lifestyle choices that are conducive to successful living through effective personal relationships, professional development, and spiritual grounding."

It required new levels of leadership and responsibility, and I was trying to figure it out. I didn't know anything about what I was getting ready to do. Everything was about learning, developing, and growing. I went to work on all the licensing requirements, hiring staff, and learning all the aspects of that type of business. It wasn't easy. I was employing nurses, doctors, and counselors. I didn't have a manual that told me the starting salaries or average pay for these positions, but I embraced the challenge.

I may not know how to do something at first, but I never let not knowing how to do something prevent me from doing it when I put my mind to it. My vision of seeing people get to the same place in life that I was in has always helped me figure things out.

As I labored to get New Day ready to open, Kristin was in a professional transition of her own that was arguably far more emotionally difficult than mine. When she became pregnant again, her mom was in the process of closing her dad's company. It had been around for two generations, dating back to her grandfather. Then, just before New Day was scheduled to open in October 2012, the Lord again spoke to Kristin.

"Just as I asked Doug to come to New Day," God told her, "I'm going to ask if you will help him." She'd been working for her parents her entire adult life. Being the oldest, she felt responsible for her mother and brother. She said it was like leaving home all over again, but the Lord had told her that as long as she was at that business, her mother wouldn't sell it.

My wife obeyed God, leaving the only job she'd ever had to work with me in this new place where the electricity hadn't even been turned on and we didn't have any money.

Kristin stopped working for her mother right as New Day officially opened. She had a bachelor's degree in social work from the University of Louisiana Monroe, completing her final semester right after her father's death. So, Kristin took care of the billing department at New Day along with whatever else people needed help doing—including conducting counseling sessions with our clients. She was incredible.

Kristin said she'd always had a heart for our clients to know Jesus. She taught them how to hear the voice of the Lord for themselves. "It was just a really beautiful time," she said. "I had my bachelor's in social work, so I thought, 'Why not? I can get a bunch of people together and talk. I can do that all day.'"

But that wasn't all. Kristin did everything from making name badges for the employees and fulfilling administrative and billing duties to case management work where she obtained the clinical information to acquire the authorizations needed to treat the clients. "I just saw a need and I would step in and help," Kristin said. "I wasn't given a named position. I have always been 'Miss Kristin' or 'Doug's wife.' I never asked for a title. They call me their spiritual advisor."

It was different having Kristin as a co-worker. I'm a task master, and I quickly learned that she was not just another person who needed to be tasked by me. Kristin often told me, "Baby, that's not how a marriage works. That's not how a relationship works." Yet she later said, "Doug and I just have a deep, deep love for each other, so we both do whatever we have to do to make it work."

~~~~

All of that was going on in the midst of the pregnancy. Our emotions were heightened, and it was a whole new level of stress. We lived our lives in trimesters, each one associated with how much energy Kristin did or didn't have or how good she did or didn't feel. Work was very stressful because there was so much going on, but we still had faith as we carefully, and at times fearfully, counted down to the birth of our child.

Because her blood pressure was a bit high, Kristin was placed on bedrest two weeks before the birth as a precaution. In February 2013, Kristin had a Cesarean section, necessary because the doctors said her pelvis wasn't big enough for the size of the baby. At first, she wasn't in favor of having a C-section. Kristin really wanted natural childbirth, but she said the Lord told her to trust Him because He saw something that she didn't. That was true. The umbilical cord ended up wrapped around the baby's neck. A natural birth would have cut off oxygen to the child's lungs.

The procedure was successful, Kristin had a boy, and he weighed in at seven pounds, six ounces. We named him Michael Douglas after her dad and me—and we'll never forget when they cleaned him up, put him in a blanket, and gave him to me to hand to Kristin. He was crying, but when she said his name, he immediately quieted, turned his head toward her, and nuzzled his cheek to hers. "Oh my gosh, he recognizes my voice," Kristin said later as she recalled the moment. It was amazing.

Kristin took the next two months off from work, and it was a good thing because there were complications. After they got home, Kristin would tremble, her body shaking from head to toe. She didn't know what was happening, but when she called the doctor the next day, they told her it was normal. The trembling was a response to the shock of childbirth. She was also unable to successfully breast feed, in part because the milk wouldn't draw (she was told that, too, was normal) and also because Michael would get a glazed-over look whenever it was time for him to suckle. We didn't know what was going on at first, and it made Kristin feel like a failure.

Then, when Doo Dee was over, she noticed something all too familiar.

"Kristin, you need to take him to the hospital," she said. "You and your sister would do the same thing."

She believed it was seizures.

Michael was admitted and remained in the Pediatric Intensive Care Unit for the next five days. She stayed with him all day, and I relieved her at night so she could come home and rest. But the doctors couldn't find anything wrong with him. In the end, Kristin was provided a prescription for phenobarbital, which our son took for three months before being weaned off of it because he hadn't had another seizure. Then Michael had another one, and he was switched to Keppra.

When he was first placed on the phenobarbital, Kristin panicked. Her fears intensified when he kept having seizures— and she really struggled with giving Michael any medication.

"It was because the Lord had given me a promise," she later shared. "He said Michael would be healthy 'from the top of his head to the bottom of his feet.' Well, he came out with seizures, so obviously he was not that healthy. That was my perception. I had to give this child medicine even though God said he would be healthy. I needed Him to help me understand why. Finally, God helped me to see that Michael *was* healthy, but that something was maturing within his biological processes. I needed to give him the medicine by faith, not because he wasn't healthy."

Despite the medications, the doctors could not pinpoint why the seizures were happening. Everything they did, from electroencephalograms (EEGs) to blood work, never showed anything. It seemed like the seizures were related to some sort of dehydration, but a definitive cause was never identified.

Another challenge arose when we were encouraged to stop trying to breast feed Michael but to give him formula instead. We went through seven different formulas before we found one that didn't upset his stomach. It was so frustrating. On top of that, Michael didn't really start sleeping all night until eight weeks in. The phenobarbital was keeping him awake, and I'd walk him indoors and out, bounce him, and sing baby rhyme raps for hours every night. I can tell you, I sometimes wished I could have had some of that phenobarbital. It was summertime, the sun didn't go down until nine o'clock, and I'd be out there fighting mosquitos while trying to get him to go to sleep.

When Kristin returned to work at New Day, if Michael wasn't with Doo Dee, he was with Kristin at work. After starting on the Keppra, things seemed to be settling down a bit until Michael contracted a bad stomach virus on New Year's Eve. "He hadn't had a seizure in I don't know how long," Kristin said, "and then he got the virus, became dehydrated, and it threw him into having another seizure. This one was so bad his lips turned blue, and Doug was trying to give him CPR." Kristin ran next door to a neighbor who was a nurse, and she was able to get Michael breathing again.

Such were our scares when Michael was small, and at one point he was actually diagnosed with epilepsy, but we refused to receive it. "When the doctor came in and said that was what Michael had," Kristin recalls, "Michael took a plate of food he was eating and threw it on the floor at the doctor." She said it was Michael's way of showing the doctor what he thought of the diagnosis.

"On our last appointment following numerous follow-up visits, we took Michael in for a final evaluation. The doctor asked, 'Who said this child has epilepsy?' Doug and I both said, 'You did!' He said, 'I don't remember saying that. This child has no signs of epilepsy.'"

Michael remained on Keppra until he was three, and he hasn't had a seizure since. By then, a neurosurgeon had advised us that dehydration from a lack of calcium, sodium, and potassium was the likely culprit behind the seizures.

As he grew into a toddler, and we continued our work at New Day, we went through the typical transitions of being a married couple and parents. As Kristin put it, "Everybody has that moment where they are like, 'Okay, nobody is coming to get this kid,' and 'I'm not even sure if I like my husband anymore,' and 'I don't think it's going to work,' and so on."

I used to go to the gym to work out in the early evening, but that came to an end real quick. "He would be gone all day long, and then he would leave work and go to the gym, while I was at home with a newborn." Kristin remembered. "Are you kidding me?" She told me one time, so the next morning I got up at four o'clock to begin working out then.

I told her, "Baby, you are a little bit younger than me, and I need to stay in shape and fit."

We laugh about that, and so many other adjustments, today, but we made the transition through all of them.

~~~~

Another significant event in our marriage happened about two months after Michael was born. There was a Christian outreach program about 45 minutes away in Winnsboro, Louisiana that New Day had partnered with called Fresh Start. Every other Thursday, me and a good buddy of mine, Donnie Williams, would go down there to preach or teach.

Donnie came up with an idea to take a group of our clients to do a special encounter event on a Friday night and return on Saturday. Friday was a church service/pep rally to try to create excitement about what we were going to do the next day. Then, on Saturday, we broke off into groups of about eight men each. Each group was assigned a leader, and in that more intimate gathering, we shared our deepest, darkest secret, something we had never told anybody else. After that, everyone came back together for a big chapel service, and the day concluded with a fish fry that wives, girl-friends, and friends and family members could attend.

I immediately knew my secret. It was something I had remembered but never shared with anyone, and it had been stirred up within me, in part, by Kristin's past traumas.

It happened when I was seven while we were living in Wichita Falls. That was the last place our family was together before the drugs, drinking, and infidelity resulted in my parents breaking up. Back then, I think just about every man in America had a subscription to Playboy, Hustler, or Penthouse. Of course, my dad had those magazines and, of course, I had looked at them, even at such a young age.

My sister, Penny, had a friend of hers over one night, and that friend molested me. It was one or two in the morning, my parents were asleep, and I vividly remember struggling to turn on the water in the bathroom to wash off after it happened. I felt so nasty.

But that wasn't the first incident. One year earlier, after a drunken party, a family member who had passed out on the couch insinuated that I should have sex with her. I didn't do it, but I remember how it made me feel—the whole shameful, lustful thought behind it—and I carried it, and the later actual molestation, with me as a secret.

Like Kristin did with the abuse she suffered, I believe I repressed all of it. Today, though, I'm convinced those incidents, even repressed, were at the root of my promiscuity as a young man. It wasn't until after I got out of prison that all of a sudden, and out of nowhere, I began remembering bits and pieces of what had happened, with fuller memory coming later in conjunction with the revelation of Kristin's abuses. I just couldn't bring myself to tell anybody.

Then came that small group session. Everyone shared their secrets. Some talked about drinking at the lake or stealing a car. Others shared how they had murdered someone. It was heavy stuff.

Then I shared my memory with these men, some of whom I had never met before in my life. I related all the details and how I had kept it secret for 36 years, all the way from the time I was six years old. It had me bound up, and I found myself thinking about it all the time, especially after Kristin had told me about her experiences. But I still hadn't told her. I was just so ashamed. *Surely, if I tell my wife,* I thought, *she might not love me. She might not be attracted to me. She might not want to have sex with me. She might want to leave me, thinking I'm ruined.*

I revealed all of that to those men.

Still surprised by what I had just done, I was asked to be the speaker at the chapel service to a much larger group of about 150 people. I'll never forget it. I got up there, and I had decided to talk about The Parable of the Prodigal Son from Luke 15. I taught about the voices that we hear—the

Father's voice, the Son's voice, and then the voice of the Holy Spirit—and as I did, that same Spirit told me to tell the crowd everything I had shared in small group.

Without hesitation, I obeyed. It was powerful. I had never felt as *light* as I did after I shared my secret with them.

When I got home that afternoon after the fish fry, I knew what I had to do next. I was excitedly scared to tell Kristin—yet she was so *happy* for me when I told her. That was the last response I expected to get from her, I was so nervous and frightened, but I was set free because I was no longer concerned about shame causing me to keep the secret that had been tormenting me and leaving me powerless.

Before that day, Kristin would ask me to tell her about my childhood, and I'd give such surface responses. "It was fine." "It was great." Stuff like that. But my brother, Mark, had apparently told her stories that obviously didn't match up with what I told her.

I guess I remembered it how I *wanted* to remember it. It was incredible to finally feel liberated enough to tell Kristin about how it really was.

Again, my wife was simply amazing. "When he shared with me, the first thing I said to myself was, 'thank goodness,' because that could have easily come up later. I know sexual abuse has a way of doing that. If you don't deal with it, it makes you kind of strange," Kristin said. "Doug usually doesn't share his emotions, feelings, or anything like that. It's not that he is numb or aloof, but he is pretty stable, and he is usually at peace."

"I can remember when I shared my abuse with him, and I asked him if he had ever been sexually abused. He said, 'No, I don't think so.' I believed him at the time, and I think he was really being truthful. It was just something that he had stuffed down," she said. "I was glad that it was something the enemy couldn't use to try to torment him. I was thankful that he shared it with me, too, because he didn't have to. It's vulnerable and intimate. I was honored."

I had continued meeting with Kevin every Friday morning. He talked to me as a son, as a brother, as a friend, as a businessman, as a Christian, and as a leader. He showed me aspects and attributes of God that I never realized before. Still, the most transformation happened for me spiritually when Kristin and I started doing a monthly Night of Encounter at our large meeting space at New Day.

It was originally conceived after Kristin's very personal and supernatural encounter with the Holy Spirit following the miscarriage. "I remember during that week saying that I wanted to have a space where I could invite people to experience what I was experiencing with God," Kristin said. "A few years later, I heard the Lord say, 'It is time for you to start dreaming about what you dreamed about that day.' I started thinking about having a place where people could come, worship, and really encounter the genuine presence of God. Then one day He said, 'Go ask Doug if you can have the big room.' When I did, he said, 'Oh, babe, that'd be awesome.'"

We didn't want it to compete with any other events or activities that churches had going on, so we scheduled it to occur one Friday each month, the first Friday if possible. We wanted it to have a freshness and create a hunger and desire in people so they would want to come back for more. We usually had up to 100 people show up each time, maybe 20 guys from New Day and the rest from the community. It was packed.

Generally, I opened with prayer and then went right into worship. Sometimes we found ourselves worshipping for two hours before anything else happened. If somebody had a testimony, or something else they wanted to say, they were allowed to share, and people told us the presence of God was so thick, it was apparent He was there, touching people's hearts.

It was so magical to me to have somebody testify about something that it made me just come alive. It was more moving than anything I read in the Bible because the accounts came with real-life application. Those nights allowed me the opportunity to block everything else out and really connect with God in a completely different way than I did at church. There was a freedom, a liberty, to experience and encounter the Lord.

Kristin said that she experienced such a sweet presence at the encounters. "Just to look out into the room and see the desire that was birthed out of me in such a place of pain—to see it come about for other people to be able to encounter Him in their places, wherever they were—was humbling, but really cool," she said.

Those nights contributed to what was also happening spiritually in our marriage. As Kristin puts it, she and I were learning to constantly, in and out of every season and in every day, cultivate the presence of God. "It is hard to fight when you have worship music constantly on in your house," she said. "It is hard to be mad at each other when you are constantly giving thanks and rejoicing. Not that we are perfect. We are human, very human. But it is something that we both desired."

~~~~~

We were still learning and growing in God when, right before Michael was two, Kristin heard from God once again.

"It's time." He announced.

"Time for what?" she asked.

God said, "Your body is ready to carry another child."

"The Lord is so cool like that," Kristin said. "I had to go to Doug and once again say, 'Okay, it's time.' I wasn't scared to make love that time."

Within a month, Kristin was pregnant—and we both knew this was going to be different than it was the last time. "With Michael's pregnancy, the Lord reassured me, just like a father would do after a daughter has a loss. But I remember Him saying, 'With this one, Kristin, you are going to have to learn to keep me in the mystery,'" she said.

Eight weeks in, Kristin began bleeding, and we went to the doctor. The baby's heartbeat was steady, but the doctor wouldn't make any promises that another miscarriage wouldn't happen. We were devastated. When I asked Kristin how she felt, she pulled no punches.

"I feel like the Lord just lied to me."

"You know what, baby," I replied tenderly. "We have a strong heartbeat, and that is where we are going to anchor our faith."

We made up our minds that God was going to keep His promise.

When we went back a couple of days later to get another ultrasound, the technician asked why we were there. Kristin told her that she'd had a lot of bleeding in her uterus and felt like she was preparing for a miscarriage.

The technician said there was absolutely no trace of blood in her uterus.

"That was a really cool moment," Kristin said, "but after going through that, we were only given two more ultrasounds because of insurance. I really had to lean in and trust. I had to find a place of rest through the pregnancy."

I focused on helping Kristin differently than I did the first time around. Back then, I was there to provide reassurance and try to take whatever responsibilities I could off her plate. The second time, I really called on her to move forward in faith. Pregnancy was hard for her. She really didn't enjoy being pregnant. But we dealt with everything as a team, and we relied on God a lot more as a couple. Our relationships, with Him and with each other, were definitely deeper.

In February 2015, there was a rare snowstorm heading into northern Louisiana when Kristin got a call from the hospital regarding her scheduled C-section. "Can you be here in 30 minutes to have your baby? Because of the storm, everybody either moved or cancelled their appointments."

She agreed, and when we arrived, there was only one other mother there to give birth. The only hiccup in the procedure came when the anesthesiologist, who was new to the hospital, took a half hour to find the right spot for the shot to initiate the spinal block for the C-section to begin. "She kept shooting it in me," Kristin recalled, "and my leg would be numb. Everywhere she hit, it was like the wrong nerve or something. I'd say, 'Lady, my leg is numb,' and she would say, 'Oh, is it?'"

Frustrating as that was, Kristin said it was nice and quiet with most everyone else gone because of the storm, and the rest of the procedure went perfectly. When Kristin returned to the recovery room, she looked out the window to see snow on the tree branches and big flakes falling from the sky.

"It was a 'happy' from God," Kristin said, "something we could always talk about from the day she was born."

The baby was a girl, seven pounds, four ounces, and we named her Hadley Grey after her grandmother Doo Dee's middle name. "I'd always had a desire to have a boy and a girl, and I wanted the boy to be first," Kristin said. "I don't know why, but I just thought it would be a better for the boy to be first. So, it was. She was a little girl."

Of course, we kept an eye out for the possibility that Hadley could have seizures just like Michael did, but she had no problems at all the first couple of days. On the third day, as she was about ready to be discharged, Kristin saw something in Hadley's eyes that just didn't look right. She told the nurse.

"No," the nurse replied, "we took her back and observed her, and she's got gas."

Kristin was blunt. "Look, lady. I'm telling you I know what this is, and I'm not leaving until you observe her a little bit more." She remembered looking out the window. The snow was long gone, and the skies were a brilliant blue. "Lord," Kristin said to the heavens, "if this is what I think it is, I need you to do something about it. Make a way so that she can go to the baby NICU and not pediatric intensive care where there is flu and sickness."

Immediately, alarms went off in the hospital, and other nurses came running into the room. Confused, Kristin asked what was going on.

"They said that as soon as they went to discharge Hadley, it came up that someone was trying to steal her. The whole floor shut down. I looked at the nurse and said, 'Now, will you go observe my baby?' She said, 'Yes, ma'am, I will.'"

They took Hadley, observed her, and transferred her to the NICU, where she stayed for the next five days.

An explanation was never given about the alarm or its cause, but it was obvious no one was trying to steal Hadley. To this day, we believe it was God intervening for us in a rather strange and spectacular way.

Every test imaginable was run on Hadley. Nothing was found. Because she was so healthy, they told us they kept her just to be thorough. "We don't see what you were talking about," the doctor said, "but we took her in on your word." Once again, they decided to discharge Hadley.

Kristin remained unconvinced. She prayed again. "Lord, I know that I know it, so you are going to have to show them."

Then, just as Hadley was about to be released, the doctors went running into her room. "The nurses came and said, 'Y'all can't come back here now. She is having what you said she was having,'" Kristin said. "I thanked God. Once again, they were trying to discharge her, and I told the Lord He would have to take over because they weren't listening to me."

During and after her treatment, Kristin spent her time visiting the other babies and their mothers in the NICU. "I would come and visit Hadley, and they would ask what was wrong with her because she looked so healthy. She was the biggest baby in there. The other babies were two or three pounds. They were little sick babies. I said, 'You know, Lord, I'm not going to let the enemy steal this from me. I'm going to just start praying for people.' I knew Hadley was okay, but they were going to do all these tests to make sure," Kristin said. "I knew it was the same thing Michael had."

Nevertheless, when Hadley was finally released, no clear diagnosis was given. Again, they simply took us at our word, and she was placed on phenobarbital.

Hadley had only a couple more seizures after that. They were less dramatic than Michael's, and she was off the medication within six months. She hasn't a seizure since.

Being a girl, Hadley's needs were so different from Michael's. Literally, all she wanted as a baby was to be carried, and she did wake up throughout the night for an entire year. She still likes sleeping with us whenever we allow it. From the very beginning, even before she could talk, we could tell she had a personality. As she's grown into a little girl, I've told Kristin, "That girl is going to be famous. I can see it. I can hear it."

Hadley is warm and compassionate, but also very humorous. She is a loving, caregiver type of person. She is definitely a Type A personality, too. When Hadley was three-and-a-half, she was communicating like a five-year-old. She has a good vocabulary. She is articulate. She's the perfect complement to Michael's personality. He's a learner, the kind of person who wants to know the details about how to do something, and the whole time we are explaining it to him, he's already planning how he is going to do it. Michael also has faith. One time, Kristin and I were talking about how people sometimes blame God for getting them sick. Michael said, "God would not do that." He just *believed* it. Finally, he is a boy of trust and integrity. He is not going to lie or sneak off to get something he is not supposed to have. Like Hadley, Michael is loving and kind.

We are so proud of both of our children, and we are blessed they are in our lives.

Kristin and I got along better as a couple in Hadley's early years than we did with Michael, even though we went from having one child to two. Michael was still a toddler then, so we had to figure out how to have time for each other. Meanwhile, New Day went into a constant pattern of growth in the years after Hadley's birth. It went from being a mom-and-pop organization to something that was definitely bigger and more streamlined. Our clientele and services increased, as did our impact on the community.

It was a hectic, exciting time in our lives. God had done so many incredible thing in and through us. We had started and grown our family.

All was going well.

But there was a new countdown underway.

My next pardon hearing was coming up in 2016—and we had no idea what to expect.

CHAPTER TEN

DEFINING MOMENTS
AND A "NEW" NEW DAY

IT SEEMED LIKE AN ETERNITY HAD PASSED since my arrest all those years ago on possession of cocaine, benzodiazepines, GHB, and marijuana, all with the intent to distribute. Equally distant was my day in court—the day I told the judge that I was not going to be serving time, but it was going to serve me—but I never forgot it or what I said as I stared down my prison term.

"I am going to learn all that I can," I said, "and be a success story for you."

Since then, I had discovered that real success was indeed measured by the decisions and the actions I made, by seeing each obstacle as an opportunity, and by moving toward the destiny before me.

But I still had one piece of unfinished business.

From my very first year in prison, I had tried to secure a pardon. Getting one involved going before a risk review board, a three-person panel that had within its power the ability to recommend me to receive a pardon which would forgive my crime and restore my voting rights, among other benefits. The board's main responsibility was to determine whether or not I was a risk to be considered for clemency or early parole.

I went before the board the first time fully persuaded that I was going to get a pardon. That was how much I believed in myself and in due process.

Was I ever wrong. That first hearing included a person who was the assistant secretary of the Louisiana Department of Corrections. The panel grilled me for 25 minutes, interrogating me about my charges and the drugs. The assistant secretary made himself an enemy from the get-go.

"What do you call this GHB?" he challenged.

I knew what he wanted me to say. But I didn't say it.

He was incensed. "Don't you think we know what it is called? It is the date rape drug."

"With all due respect," I responded, "I'm sure that is what you call it, but you asked me what I call it. That is not what I call it because I never used it for that."

I lost that hearing—and the three that followed it over the next several years. It wasn't until five years into my sentence that I finally got a recommendation for a pardon hearing, but that assistant secretary wasn't pleased about it. "You are getting a recommendation," he said snidely, "but it was not unanimous."

Of course, God had done a lot of work in my life by then, so I determined that I was going to do something to bless that man because he had made himself my enemy. I ended up making him a plaque for the door of his office. It was shaped like the state of Louisiana, and it had our state emblem with the pelican seal on it along with his official title and his credentials.

I gave it to him one day when he visited the Forcht-Wade Correctional Center. I don't know if he was there on his regular rounds to the different prisons, or if he was there to see his nephew who was incarcerated at the prison. Either way, when I gave it to him, he thanked me, then asked, "Did you make this?"

I told him I did. I hoped he would see it as evidence that I wasn't who he thought I was.

I didn't see him again until years later when I was working at the McDonald's in Ruston. He came in one day, and when I recognized him, I made a point of waiting on him and brought him his lunch. I told him my name and asked if he remembered me. He said he did. I think I caught him off guard. He didn't say anything else other than "thank you."

After my sentence was recalculated and I was released in late 2010, I took the recommendation I had received all those years earlier from the risk review board and applied for clemency.

I was shot down. I received a form letter in the mail in 2012, stating that I was denied because of the nature of my crime and that I had not served enough time on my sentence.

The same thing happened two years later.

By 2016, I truly believed I had the best chance ever at securing the pardon. It had been six years since I had been out of prison. I only had about three-and-a-half years left on my parole. My life was good. I was married and had children. I had long-term stability in my employment. Things seemed to be on my side, and I even garnered the help of Louisiana state representative Jack McFarland to try and make it happen.

Even then, I thought back to a phone call I had with my dad after my first hearing. I recalled telling him that I just knew I was going to get a pardon, adding that I could be patient about it if I had to be. "Well, son," my father said, "I've known you a really long time, and I've never known you to be patient. But you've actually been patient on this."

Patience and a good dose of persistence had indeed brought me through. With every rejection, I hadn't allowed my disappointment to carry into the next day. By that point, I had done 75 percent of my sentence. I had no violations. I hadn't failed a drug screen. I had never been arrested. I had checked all the boxes I thought proved I was a productive citizen. I believed that I had a story that supported my rehabilitation efforts.

If it could happen to someone else, it could happen to me. Why not me!

Representative McFarland ended up going to bat for me big time. When the day came for my case to be reviewed by the pardon board, he spoke to the chairperson on my behalf, monitored it for me personally—and called me that night with the news.

I'd been shot down once more.

I was beside myself. "What more do I have to do?" I lamented. "Is there any more that I can do? Not only am I not on drugs and alcohol, but I am helping people *get off* of drugs and alcohol."

Then he told me something else. "I talked to the lady who was the head of the board. She said she looked at your case and your charges and couldn't figure out why you got a 20-year sentence to begin with. She said you should try to go back to court. She said you should get a pardon, but because you were still on parole, they couldn't give you a pardon."

I was shocked. Nowhere in any of the documentation I had did it ever say that.

But I knew I had to remain patient and persistently keep moving forward.

Louisiana Governor John Bel Edwards entered office in January 2016 with a priority of criminal justice reform. He signed legislation in 2017 that targeted recidivism and invested in treatment programs like the one at New Day. By 2018, the state had seen a 20-percent decrease in the number of people imprisoned for non-violent crimes.

Re-elected to a second term in 2019, I decided to reapply in February 2020. Right after I turned in an online application for a pardon hearing, the COVID-19 pandemic hit. Almost six months later, I got a letter in the mail saying that my request for a pardon had been granted, adding that the process could take about a year. In the meantime, it instructed me to get people to write letters on my behalf in advance of a future final hearing on the matter.

I had never stopped believing I was going to get a pardon, even after every rejection. I just felt like God had spoken into my heart that I was going to get one. This book was published before that hearing took place. But I never stopped believing.

~~~~~

Another challenge came when the Louisiana state statutes were revised in 2016 with a clause that said a person cannot be a chief executive officer, administrator, director, or manager if they had ever been convicted of a felony for drugs or alcohol. That meant I couldn't be any of those things unless I had completed my parole by a minimum of five years and been sober for two years by personal attestation. I was good on that count, but I was still on parole.

All I could think was, *Now I'm gonna have to give up my job?*

Yet I knew the Lord didn't want me to lose my job. He had me at New Day for a reason, and He'd called me to do it. Still, the possibility that something could happen came with a lot of mental anguish and turmoil, and I really didn't know what to do about it until I reached out to another state representative, Katrina Jackson. I met with her at her office in Monroe, and I even tried to hire her to review my legal case. That was tricky, in that she had two divisions: her legal office and her representative office. I couldn't go in and talk to her about my case if I was talking to her as the state representative and vice versa.

In the end, I chose not to pursue the legal case, but she still helped me with the process of presenting my situation to the Louisiana Department of Health and Hospitals. When she finally got an answer from the state, Representative Jackson told me the law couldn't be changed, but since I'd been at New Day for a long time, I could keep my position there—as long as nobody made a big issue out of it. Once my pardon was granted, the law would no longer be a threat.

Since then, only once did someone threaten to rat me out. How did I respond? "The state already knows I'm here, so go ahead and turn me in." The person never did—but the old me would have tried to cover it up and cower away in hiding. It was just another indication of everything the Lord had been doing in my life that I chose to see it the way I did.

Then, in 2017, Kristin decided to pursue a master's degree in social work, and having that degree has proven to be favorable for her. "The space that opened up for me, not only financially, but to have different opportunities to be able to do what I enjoy doing—the degree backs it up. I can legally do what I want to do, and nobody can tell me I can't," Kristin said. "As a woman, it is a lot different than it is for Doug. He will probably never have to have a degree, but for women it is different. My degree sets me apart because I am a woman. Others can't be discriminating against me because I have the degree."

"I remember the Lord telling me that. He said, 'Kristin, you do have credibility in the spirit, but this will give you credibility in the world.'"

All of that is true—but Kristin's master's degree didn't change how much I already highly esteemed her. I have always looked at her as being able to do whatever she wants. I was just cheering her on because I already saw she could do it.

~~~~~

On September 5, 2019, I completed my 20-year sentence and parole. By then, I had been running New Day on parole for seven years.

That was a Thursday, and in the weekly group session I conducted that day with the guys at New Day, I talked to them about finishing what you start and finishing well.

"When you want something so bad," I taught, "and it is so far away, it seems impossible. It's like you are never going to get there. There's this story of two people mining for gold. One guy was digging and digging, and he stopped a foot before he got to the jackpot. The other guy dug and dug, and he broke through. How many times do we stop before we get to where we want to go, do what we want to do, or become what we are trying to become? We never really know how close we were because we stopped."

Kristin and I didn't do anything special to celebrate that night. I considered posting a video on Facebook about it but chose not to. It's funny. I'd waited 20 years to get to that day, and I thought it would be the biggest celebration party ever.

But we didn't do that. There wasn't any justification for it.

We knew we still weren't finished doing what the Lord had called us to do.

There is no doubt that everything leading up to that point has made us into the people we are today. My wife has taught me how to overcome my fears and realize that we don't let shame, guilt, or condemnation cause us to think any certain way about one another, the love she has for me, or the love I have for her. I will say that I have always seen more of who Kristin is than she has been able to believe of herself, but I can still tend to be a bit too emphatic with her. "Sometimes Doug just needs to realize that I need a gentle reminder to affirm me," she said. "Most of the time, it is not that easy for me to just see something then move on to the next thing. I'm more of a crock pot than a microwave."

In our journey as a couple, Kristin and I are always side by side, but one of us has continually pulled the other one ahead. We challenge each other. We are always paying attention to what the other one says. When she challenges me, I may not acknowledge it right away, but by the time she gets up the next morning I will have gone before God and listened to the Holy Spirit.

"Doug is incredibly steady and stable," Kristin said. "He wasn't always like that in the beginning of our marriage. He wasn't as self-controlled as he is today as far as being able to refrain from feeling like he has to prove himself. Early on, Doug would defend himself, and I had to convince him that I wasn't trying to accuse him of anything. Now he is confident and at ease. He doesn't have to fight for his position. He doesn't have to prove that he is never again going to be the man that he was before. The growth he's made is leaps and bounds."

Kristin recalls Psalm 37:6. "It says, 'He will make your righteous reward shine like the dawn, your vindication like the noonday sun.' I would tell Doug, 'That's what you are: the righteousness of God in Christ.' When I first shared that with Doug, he told me, 'Babe, that's what I used to tell myself in prison.' I had no idea. It was just really cool."

It was, and still is. Kristin and I are growing, maturing, and developing. I was a guy who lied, cheated, stole, cussed, and slept around. Falling in love with the Lord—and falling in love with my wife in this pure way—has given me single vision for her and for what God is now doing in us and through us.

~~~

This book is filled with defining moments that have helped me make changes in my life that I had never been able to make before. The lessons I have learned from those moments have given me hope and enabled me to transform my identity and self-worth.

In 2021, Kristin and I launched **Your New Day with Doug and Kristin Pollock**. It was birthed from our desire to motivate others—specifically those dealing with addiction and couples in struggling marriages—to discover their defining moments and maximize them to change their lives.

The Lord first led us to do this shortly after we were married and attended marriage conferences that helped us see what we needed to work on in our relationship. Not only

were we drawn to marriage ministry, but we envisioned ourselves being able to do the same thing. By the time I began
formally writing *Why Not Me!* in fall 2019, the seed had been
planted in our hearts. It has since sprung into a full-fledged,
for-profit ministry where we use speaking events, work-
shops, and special encounters to motivate others to discover
their life's defining moments, find hope, and transform their
identity and self-worth.

As a couple, we have overcome a variety of personal
challenges, some of which you experienced with us in this
book. Each one created defining moments that caused us to
break free of our past hurts and move forward into all that
God has for us. Today, Kristin and I find peace and power
from our relationships with God and with each other, and
our desire is to help others be free from the issues of their
past, so they can strengthen themselves and their most trea-
sured relationships.

We are literally overflowing with lessons God has taught
us that we want to pass on to others. For example, we want
people to *see the value of who they are* instead of diminish-
ing their skill, position in life, or disposition in life. Through
God, they can view themselves and their opportunities in a
different way. People can also find their own significance and
allow that realization to change how they view themselves
and others. They will only see their value when they have a
proper definition of who they are.

Kristin and I also believe that all of us need to have an
honest talk with ourselves to discover if we are living up to
the best version of who we want to be. When we do this, we
can easily find out if we like who we are and are satisfied
with the life we are currently living. If we're not, then we
have to *write a new definition.* We encourage people to think
about their lives from three perspectives: their past, their
present, and their future. It is through those perspectives that
they can come up with a definition that will propel them to
where they want to be.

One of the challenges we face in life is getting into a rut. Everyone's rut looks a bit different. Sometimes it is evidenced by how we feel. Other times, it's manifested by the messages we choose to tell ourselves over and over. Some of these things you just can't escape, but escaping is not the answer. Instead, the solution is figuring out how to face these issues head on because it's often what we do in the midst of our greatest trials that causes us to turn our lives around. The truth is, we get to where we are one thought at a time. If we can begin to unpack the lies we have come to believe and replace them with truth, we can climb out of our "RUT" by 1) *Regaining* the ability to take back what we believe we have lost, 2) doing it in an *Undeniable* way so that we cannot be convinced otherwise, and 3) realizing that while there may be many facts, *Truth* is truth.

Finally, one of Kristin's biggest passions that she will address with women through Your New Day with Doug and Kristin Pollock is the lie that "I can't." She believes that when it comes to hurt, "it always seems too painful to process or even talk about. It's vulnerable and intimate, and there is always a risk of, 'If I let you see me, what will you do with what I'm entrusting you with? How do I know you won't expose my shame or leave me alone in it?'"

"Most of my experiences have proven that no one can be trusted with my most intimate parts, not even me. So, since this is what I believe about myself and the people around me, I will take matters into my own hands, and I will hide those parts away from everyone, even myself," Kristin said. "My message to these women is *you absolutely can*. You can heal, let go, forgive, and most importantly, be seen right where you are, in the exact condition you are in."

"Being willing to look at yourself invites the process of recognizing the beauty of yourself. It teaches you how to embrace the wonder of looking at yourself only with love and acceptance. From this place, you begin to live the truest version of yourself: fully seen, fully accepted, and fully loved," she said.

In the end, Kristin and I are convinced that people need hope, and finding and living in hope produces character. Many times, when we feel we are stuck in the bottom of a hole, it's easier to stay stuck than it is to figure out how to climb out. There are things that we have spent our lives saying or believing that trap us, but God wants to expand who we believe we are created to be. As we mentally and spiritually get to the place where doing whatever it takes literally means "whatever it takes," hope is infused within us and our character is built.

For those who are courageous enough to believe *Why Not Me!* for themselves, the results are limitless. They can see marriages restored, experience freedom from addiction, and develop a new perspective from the mistakes they have made. A transformed life filled with optimism and opportunity is theirs for the taking as they trust in God and allow Him to change them.

Made in the USA
Columbia, SC
28 December 2021

51506336R00133